Whining Doesn't Win

Whining Doesn't Win

Ben Shapiro

Creators Publishing
Hermosa Beach, CA

WHINING DOESN'T WIN
Copyright © 2019 CREATORS PUBLISHING

Cover art by Peter Kaminski

CREATORS PUBLISHING
737 3rd St
Hermosa Beach, CA 90254
310-337-7003

Although the author and publisher have made every effort to ensure that the information in this book was correct at press time, the author and publisher do not assume and hereby disclaim any liability to any party for any loss, damage or disruption caused by errors or omissions, whether such errors or omissions result from negligence, accident or any other cause.

ISBN (print): 978-1-949673-11-1
ISBN (ebook): 978-1-949673-10-4

First Edition
Printed in the United States of America
1 3 5 7 9 10 8 6 4 2

A Note From the Publisher

Since 1987, Creators has syndicated many of your favorite columns to newspapers. In this digital age, we are bringing collections of those columns to your fingertips. This will allow you to read and reread your favorite columnists, with your own personal digital archive of their work.

—Creators Publishing

Contents

America's Left in the Grip of Insanity

January 3, 2018

President Trump is unpopular. He's unpopular because he's boorish, crude and silly; he's unpopular because he has a unique capacity to turn winning news cycles into referenda on his use of Twitter. But the United States under President Trump hasn't seen any serious anti-liberty revanchism. In fact, under Trump, regulations have dropped precipitously; the economy continues its pattern of growth; and press freedoms have actually been strengthened. Despite popular opinion, women aren't on the verge of enslavement into Vice President Mike Pence's "Handmaid's Tale," nor are black Americans in danger of resegregation or political disenfranchisement.

Yet while Iranians protest against a regime that reportedly hangs homosexuals from cranes, members of the hard left in the United States insist that protesters against the Trump administration demonstrate bravery similar to that of Iranians risking death by an Islamist regime. Huffington Post political commentator Alex Mohajer tweeted: "The #IranianProtests, the #Resistance, and @WomensMarch are all the same. Across the world, people are fighting autocracies and oppressive regimes. @realDonaldTrump is NO DIFFERENT than the oppressive Ayatollahs in Iran." Oddly, that movement of solidarity hasn't prompted those who walked in the Women's March on Washington to say a single word in support of the Iranian protesters to this point.

This idiocy doesn't merely spring from hatred for Trump but from a deep-seated need to justify the Obama administration's feckless Iran policy. Thomas Erdbrink of The New York Times reported that violence broke out in Iran after the demonstrators ignored "pleas for calm from President Hassan Rouhani" and termed Rouhani — a tool of the mullahs — a "moderate." Meanwhile, one CNN anchor fretted that Trump might put a "finger on the scale" against the Iranian regime. Members of the Obama administration took to Twitter to tell Trump to be quiet (Susan Rice, former national security adviser), chide Trump for failing to take in Iranian refugees (Samantha Power, former U.N. ambassador) and suggest that American policy has nothing to do with Iran's protests (Ben Rhodes, former national security adviser and architect of the Iran nuclear deal narrative). All of these administration members did nothing as President Obama watched dissidents die in the streets in 2009, and all of them actively abetted the maximization of Iran's regional power.

Herein lies the insanity of the left. Only nutcases on the right believed that Barack Obama's governance was morally equivalent to the Iranian government. In the main, conservatives thought that Obama pursued bad policies domestically and horribly immoral foreign policies. But many on the left seem to believe that Trump is merely steps removed from the ayatollahs. The ayatollahs agree, and they use that nuttery for public-relations leverage: No wonder Ayatollah Khamenei tweeted: "The U.S. gov. commits oppression inside the U.S., too. U.S. police murder black women, men, & children for no justifiable reason, and the murderers are acquitted in U.S. courts. This is their judicial system! And they slam other countries' and our country's judicial system. #BLM."

Trump isn't Khamenei. And the only recent administration to help build Iran's power is the Obama administration. Comparing the Trump administration to Iran's regime isn't just delusional; it's insulting and counterproductive. And the only people it helps are America's enemies.

The Virtue-Signaling Anti-Virtue Crowd

January 10, 2018

Imagine it's late 2011. The world just found out about Jerry Sandusky, former assistant Penn State football coach who would be convicted of repeatedly raping children in 2012. Penn State higher-ups, in an attempt to turn the focus of the scandal away from the school, decide to turn an annual banquet into a celebration of those fighting child rape. They call up head coach Joe Paterno. They call up President Graham Spanier. They call up athletic director Tim Curley. All of them give long, brave speeches about the evils of sexual exploitation of children resulting in rousing applause from all the Penn State boosters. All the attendees wear pins showing their solidarity with molestation victims. The event is nationally televised.

You'd be disgusted, wouldn't you? You'd think to yourself, "Perhaps it isn't a good idea for a school that just became nationally renowned for one of the worst sex scandals in modern American history to preach about its commitment to the kiddies."

Now fast-forward to 2018. It's been only a few months since we found out that Hollywood megaproducer Harvey Weinstein allegedly raped multiple women, sexually abused other women and sexually harassed still more women. Each day, more and more prominent men are caught up in the net of #MeToo, the national movement to listen to the stories of abused women: Matt Lauer, Kevin Spacey, Charlie Rose, Russell Simmons, Jeffrey Tambor, Andrew Kreisberg, Louis C.K., Ed Westwick, Brett Ratner, Dustin Hoffman, Jeremy Piven, Danny Masterson and James Toback.

Yet on Sunday, Hollywood held itself a festival of virtue-signaling at the Golden Globes. All the women dressed in black in homage to the victims of a sexual harassment epidemic that has plagued Hollywood since the inception of the casting couch. The men wore "Time's Up" buttons to show solidarity. Oprah Winfrey, who was once quite close with Weinstein, gave an emotional speech in which she likened modern-day victims of sexual abuse to a black woman raped by six white men in 1944 Alabama. The cameras cut away to Meryl Streep, who once praised Weinstein as a "god" and gave a standing ovation to accused child rapist Roman Polanski. The entire crowd cheered its goodwill approximately six years after the Hollywood Foreign Press Association gave a lifetime achievement award to Woody Allen, who was credibly accused of molesting his own stepdaughter when she was 7 years old.

All of this was supposed to make us feel that Hollywood is somehow leading the charge against sexual aggression. But that's simply not true. Hollywood isn't doing anything to materially change its culture; it's simply operating out of fear of public scrutiny. When the spotlight moves on, people in Hollywood will go right back to doing what they've been doing for years: exploiting people less powerful than them. Winfrey had nothing to say about sexual misconduct in Hollywood for 30 years, even though she was the Queen of All Media; treating her as some sort of beacon of light now is simply ridiculous.

America knows posturing when it sees it. And what we're seeing now isn't bravery.

Stop Feministsplaining Sex to Men

January 17, 2018

There's a word that has become popular in feminist circles these days: "mansplaining." The word is a mashup of "man" and "explaining" and refers to men who condescendingly explain the facts of life to women. So, for example, if a man believes a woman doesn't understand directions and slowly repeats those directions to a woman, he's mansplaining and, therefore, guilty of cruelty and stupidity.

Well, feminists, it's time to stop "feministsplaining" sex to men.

The #MeToo movement has been good for America. It's good that women who have been sexually assaulted and abused are coming forward; it's good that we're finally having conversations about the nature of consent and the problems with a casual hookup culture that obfuscates sexual responsibility. But the #MeToo movement hasn't stopped there. Men are now being pilloried for the sin of taking women too literally — of not reading women's minds.

Take, for example, "Grace," an anonymous woman who went on a rotten date with comedian Aziz Ansari. According to Grace, Ansari treated her abominably: He took her to dinner, gave her white wine instead of red, pushed her to come to his apartment and then engaged in a vigorous round of sexual activities to which she apparently consented. She eventually said no — and when she did, he stopped. Later, she suggested that Ansari hadn't obeyed her "non-verbal cues" — nonverbal cues that reportedly included undressing and then voluntarily servicing Ansari.

In the aftermath, Grace felt used. So she texted Ansari, explaining to him that she felt terrible about the date. "I want to make sure you're aware so maybe the next girl doesn't have to cry on the ride home," she said.

This is feministsplaining sex. Here's the problem: The condescension isn't earned. From Grace's story, it seems she was less than clear in her nonverbal communications but she wanted Ansari to read her mind — and that when he didn't, she therefore had leeway to lecture him about his sins and, more broadly, those of all men.

It's not just Grace. Rachel Thompson of Mashable explained: "The responses to the woman's story are peppered with the word 'should.' She *should* have said no ... For many women, uttering an explicit 'no' is not as easy or straightforward as you might think." Well, as it turns out, reading minds is not quite as easy or straightforward as feminists might think. It was feminists who boiled down sexual relations to the issue of consent. Traditionalists always argued that physical intimacy and emotional intimacy ought to be linked. But they were accused of removing female agency with such linkage and condemned for "mansplaining."

How about this: no feministsplaining and no mansplaining when it comes to sex? How about we instead focus on communication between men and women? How about sexual partners demand more from one another than physical release so they aren't disappointed that they're being treated as sex objects? A system prizing love and commitment doesn't require nearly the amount of explanation as a system that dispenses with both.

What the Latest Stupid Government
Shutdown Means

January 24, 2018

On Monday, Democrats caved on their manufactured government shutdown. In an attempt to generate a groundswell of support for a legislative re-enshrinement of former President Obama's executive amnesty, Democrats filibustered a continuing resolution to fund the government. That tough stance lasted precisely three days. Then, Democrats voted overwhelmingly with Republicans to fund the government in its entirety for another three weeks.

This makes the second government shutdown in the last five years; back in 2013, the Republicans refused to fund then-President Obama's Affordable Care Act and then collapsed and fully funded it for nothing in return. That followed a government shutdown in 1995-1996 that ended after nearly a month, with Republicans receiving nothing from then-President Bill Clinton. And that government shutdown followed the one in November 1995, when Republicans received merely an agreement from President Clinton to balance the budget within seven years.

Notice a pattern? The president always wins government shutdowns. Congress never does.

Why is that? It's because Americans now buy into the urgency of funding the government fully. We've been trained for years that any government shutdown imperils us all: The zombie apocalypse is coming. The media have aided the cause of a growing government admirably here. This week, CNN ran a segment suggesting that a government shutdown could prevent us from tracking an inbound asteroid that could wipe out all life on Earth. Then we wonder why so many Americans are so deeply disturbed at the possibility of a shutdown that would allow Medicare and Social Security to operate largely unimpeded, that would allow the Veterans Affairs hospitals to remain open and military function to continue (though pay would be backlogged).

We also have been trained for years that the power of the purse is in the hands of the Congress, not the executive. That means we see the Congress as the party most responsible for passing legislation the president will sign, not the president as the party most responsible for agreeing with Congress. And that means that the president's priorities take center stage when dealing with Congress, even though the president is oftentimes the person holding up government funding.

Here, in essence, is the problem: We're addicted to government. The population is addicted to the notion that the government operates without the bumps and breaks uniquely built into the American system; the media are addicted to the daily show of government; the members of government are happy to keep spending cash and scare the life out of constituents when the spending stops.

Make no mistake: The Democrats' strategy and rationale for the government shutdown was awful. But if Americans have been so conditioned to panic regarding such shutdowns that 69 hours — 48 of them over a weekend — drive us to fever pitch, we have much bigger problems than a few lost work hours.

Can a Bad Man Be a Good President?

January 29, 2018

This week, FBI deputy director Andrew McCabe — a man who certainly should have stepped down months ago — finally resigned from his active role at the agency. McCabe had been under President Trump's fire for months given his failure to recuse himself from the Hillary Clinton email investigation despite his wife having received nearly $700,000 in campaign donations from Clinton associates during her failed Virginia state senatorial race.

Shortly after his resignation hit the headlines, another story broke from NBC News: The day after Trump fired then-FBI Director James Comey, Trump was astonished and angered to learn that Comey had been offered a flight home on an FBI airplane. He allegedly called up McCabe and reamed him for allowing it. When McCabe dissented from Trump's diatribe, Trump told McCabe that he ought to "ask his wife how it feels to be a loser," apparently referring to her election loss.

This is, to put it mildly, gross.

But Trump isn't exactly shy about his grossness. "Loser" is one of his favorite terms of art. Among other recipients of that accolade are Mark Cuban, George Will, former White House deputy chief of staff Karl Rove, actor Richard Belzer, Scottish farmer Michael Forbes, Glenfiddich scotch whiskey and the GOP as a whole. The list goes on.

All of this has been brushed off by conservatives. After all, Trump is providing some of the most conservative policy of the last half-century. Not only has he signed a massive tax cut into law but he has also slashed regulations, repealed the individual mandate, nominated conservative judges, moved the American embassy in

Israel to Jerusalem, supported the anti-Iranian alliance in the Middle East and moved to box in Russia. He has presided over massive economic growth at home and the collapse of the Islamic State group in Syria and Iraq.

Trump's list of accomplishments should seemingly answer a question with which conservatives have been struggling: Can a bad man make a good president? The answer, obviously, should be yes. What's more, the answer should have been obvious: Machiavelli suggested back in the 16th century that perhaps *only* a bad man can be a good politician. Machiavelli stated that virtue is an unrealistic and counterproductive standard for a statesman — what is needed is *virtu*, a capacity to use virtue and vice for the achievement of a specific end. Even Aristotle, a devotee of virtue, suggested that good citizens need not be good men.

All of which makes sense. Bad men make great artists. Bad men make great athletes. Saints often die in penury; sinners often die in riches.

But Trump's list of accomplishments is only half the story. That's because the office of the presidency is about more than mere accomplishments: It's about modeling particular behavior. Bill Clinton was a successful president, but he was not a good one: He drove the country apart, degraded our political discourse and brought dishonor to the White House. The same was true for President Richard Nixon. Doing good things as president does not mean being a good president. Being a good president requires a certain element of character.

And Trump's character is still lacking. Perhaps in the end, conservatives should ignore Trump's character defects and take the wins; I certainly cheer those wins. Perhaps in the end, Trump's character will poison the wins themselves; we won't know that for years. We do know, however, that if we believe the president has two roles — one as a policymaker, the other as a moral model — then President Trump can only be half-successful so long as he refuses to change himself.

On the Super Bowl and the Social Fabric

February 7, 2018

On Sunday, I attended the Super Bowl, along with my father, my business partner and the president of our company. It was an amazing event. That wasn't just because the game was terrific — although it was. It was because for all the competitive fire, for all the passion and excitement, one feeling permeated the stadium in the freezing wilds of Minnesota: love.

Yes, love.

The people in the stadium may have hated the other team, but they didn't hate one another. Patriots fans sat next to Eagles fans, and everybody got along; we all shouted ourselves hoarse when the NFL honored Medal of Honor winners, and we all stood for the national anthem. After the game, when we poured out into the arctic temperatures, barely able to move because of the throng, nobody was pushing or shoving or getting violent. Instead, people joked and laughed. After all, what was there to be truly angry about? We'd just witnessed an awesome spectacle, been party to a shared communal experience. Eagles fans mocked Pats fans; Pats fans good-naturedly shrugged it off. It may sound like a cliche, but the Super Bowl — in the stadium, at least — was just a giant party filled with Americans who loved being in America celebrating a great American cultural celebration.

Unfortunately, such experiences are becoming rarer and rarer.

I love technology; I love choice. I cut cable years ago. Then I hooked up cable again for sports and then cut it again. My entertainment choices are personalized. So are my music choices. I can download podcasts at will. I watch movies with my wife — it takes a Big Event Movie to get me to a theater. I choose whom to follow on Facebook and Twitter. All of that is fantastic — better stuff, faster, catered to my tastes! But there's a drawback: We don't have the same common cultural ground anymore, as our tastes fragment and we can pursue them more individually.

My main communal connection comes through my synagogue, but church and synagogue attendance has been dropping precipitously for years. People aren't joining sports leagues or community organizations. We're fragmenting on nearly every level. There's a problem with that: As the social fabric atomizes, we spend less time with one another. We're less likely to see one another as friends and neighbors, and more likely to see one another as bundles of positions and views we don't share. And that makes it particularly easy for us to dismiss one another as motivated by nefarious feelings, as opposed to merely being in disagreement.

Arthur Brooks of American Enterprise Institute is fond of citing a 1934 study about discrimination against Chinese-Americans. The study followed a Chinese couple as they visited hotels and restaurants across the country. They were denied service a grand total of one time. Then, study author Richard LaPiere sent questionnaires to the various establishments asking whether they'd serve a Chinese couple. All but one that responded said no.

The lesson, as Brooks notes: "People are more hostile to others in the abstract than when they meet them in person." That means we need more communal events — and that means we have to go out of our way to engage with others. We need more shared cultural experiences. That would be a good start toward rebuilding our perceptions of one another.

This Isn't Normal

February 14, 2018

You've heard the phrase over and over again: "This isn't normal." We've heard it about President Trump's rhetoric, and his Twitter usage. We've heard it about his attacks on the media, and we've heard it about his legislative ignorance. We've heard it about his running commentary on the Mueller investigation, and we've heard it about his bizarre stream-of-consciousness interviews.

There's some truth to all of this. Trump has said some incredibly awful things (e.g. his comments on Charlottesville, Virginia, and Haitians). He's not a predictable, stable genius.

All of this "non-normality," however, has resulted in ... a relatively normal situation. The economy's booming. We're on more solid foreign-policy ground than we were when President Obama was in office — by a long shot. The constitution hasn't been torn asunder. The structures of government are still in place. Trump may be toxic rhetorically, but his presidency hasn't annihilated the norms that govern our society.

The same can't be said, however, of the media institutions that seem so consumed with saving the republic from the specter of Trump. Like self-appointed superheroes so intent on stopping an alien monster that they end up destroying the entire city, our media are so focused on stopping Trump that they end up undermining both their credibility and faith in American institutions.

Take, for example, the media's coverage of North Korea at the Winter Olympics. Suddenly, the worst regime on the planet has been transformed into a cute exhibit from "It's a Small World." Those women in red forced to smile and cheer on cue? Just an example of the brilliance of revolutionary North Korean "juche" ideology. Kim

Jong Un's sister, a member of the inner cabinet of a regime that imprisons thousands of dissenters and shoots those who don't properly worship the Dear Respected? She's an example of Marxist humility and stellar diplomacy.

It's not just the media. This week, we learned that former FBI Director James Comey, former Deputy Attorney General Sally Yates, former national security adviser Susan Rice, former Vice President Joe Biden and former President Obama held a last-minute meeting at the White House to discuss the possibility of Trump-Russia collusion. At that meeting, Rice wrote in an email, Obama reportedly asked whether there was any reason "we cannot share information fully as it relates to Russia." That means that Obama asked his top staff, including the FBI, whether he could hide intelligence information from the incoming Trump team.

That amounts to a massive breach in the constitutional structure. The FBI is not an independent agency. It is part of the executive branch. The incoming Trump administration was duly elected by the American people and had every right to see all intelligence information coming from the FBI and the CIA. Yet it was the supposedly normal Obama White House exploring means of preventing that transparency.

Trump isn't a normal president. But the threat to our institutions doesn't reside only at 1600 Pennsylvania Ave. — or even primarily there. It resides with those who are willing to side with any enemy and violate every rule in order to stop the supposed threat of Trump.

'We Have to Do Something'

February 21, 2018

The gun control debate is complex. It pits rights against duties. It pits individualism against communitarianism. It pits gun owners against anti-gun activists, and law-abiding citizens against one another. Most of all, it pits "common sense" against evidence. The vast majority of gun control proponents keep talking about "common sense" gun control, as though Americans could simply blue-sky some ideas about curbing highly sporadic acts of violence and fix the problem immediately — and as though Americans were suffering from lack of will, rather than disagreement about method. That's simply not the case.

But there are things we can do.

Let's begin with the easiest thing: We can insist that our law enforcement agencies actually *enforce the law.* The Parkland, Florida, shooting occurred because the FBI failed to do its job. Not once but *twice,* the FBI was warned about the shooter. And not once but *twice,* it ignored the warnings. That isn't rare. We know that law enforcement screwed up in the South Carolina black church massacre; we know it screwed up in the Texas church massacre; we know it screwed up in San Bernardino. We know that, as of 2013, out of 48,321 cases against straw buyers — people who buy guns for others, including those who aren't legally allowed to buy them — just 44 had been prosecuted. We know that as of 2013, there were nearly 20,000 people in California alone who weren't legally allowed to own guns but owned them anyway. Giving the government more legal power to confiscate weaponry or prosecute those who are dangerous means nothing if the government blows every available opportunity.

But we can do more.

David French at National Review suggests an option: gun-violence restraining orders, or GRVOs. These would allow family members to apply for an order enabling the legal authorities to temporarily remove guns from those who are deemed to be a significant danger to themselves or others. Furthermore, we should ensure more transparency in the background-check system with regard to mental health records, and we should look to ease the regulations on involuntary commitment of the dangerously mentally ill.

We should also radically increase security in schools. I attended a Jewish high school that was regularly threatened with violence. Every student who attends that school is now checked in by security; the school has barriers on every side; armed security guards attend the campus. The same measures should be available at every public school. Complaints about the so-called school-to-prison pipeline created by the presence of law enforcement at schools seem to be overblown, according to the data — and, more importantly, it's the school's job to ensure the safety of students, not to protect students against their own criminal behavior.

These are simple measures that should be able to achieve broad agreement. But they probably won't, because it's too politically useful for the left to rail broadly about gun control. The biggest problem with the gun control debate has been its failure to boil down slogans to proposals. That problem won't be alleviated so long as the media insist on putting mourning teenagers on television with the chyron "DO SOMETHING." Something is nothing unless someone puts some actual proposals on the table.

How The Democrats Will Lose in 2020

February 28, 2018

President Trump is not a particularly popular president.

His job approval rating has not crossed 50 percent for a single day of his presidency. He's currently riding as high as he ever has in the RealClearPolitics poll average — and that's 41 percent. Statistics guru Nate Silver estimates that "the approval rating at which an incumbent candidate goes from being an underdog to a favorite for re-election is somewhere in the high 40s." Furthermore, Democrats are favored to retake the House of Representatives in 2018 — they've been dramatically outperforming their poll numbers in special elections. And there's always the possibility that the economy will tank: America has experienced an economic downturn at least once per decade for the past several decades, and our last serious downturn was in 2009.

With all of that said, Democrats can still find a way to blow this.

They could blow this in the same way they blew 2016: by picking a candidate based on intersectional concerns rather than capacity to unify Americans, and by slandering half the country.

Hillary Clinton wasn't the best candidate for president on the Democratic side of the aisle. Then-Vice President Joe Biden polled better. So, in fact, did loony Vermont Sen. Bernie Sanders. Clinton's poll numbers rarely cracked 50 percent and often veered toward 40 percent. And, of course, she was egregiously brittle, supremely inauthentic and tremendously off-putting. Yet the Democratic establishment had determined that it was, in fact, her time — with the emphasis on *her*. Clinton was a woman; her rivals weren't. We'd just elected the first black president. It was time for Clinton to break the glass ceiling. And so, the Democrats picked one of the most polarizing figures in American history to carry forward President Barack Obama's legacy.

That was Bad Decision No. 1.

Then there was Clinton's campaign. Clinton spent most of the campaign absolutely bewildered by the fact that a boorish, ignorant reality television star was running neck and neck with her. She could have taken that as a referendum on her own shortcomings. Instead, she took it as a referendum on *America's* shortcomings. America, she believed, is filled with racist, sexist, bigoted homophobes. America is a basket of deplorables. If it weren't, wouldn't she have been up 50 points?

Of course, Clinton lost.

And all indicators suggest that Democrats intend to copy her playbook.

The single most dangerous candidate to Trump's re-election is, again, Biden. Despite the fact that Biden is a pathological liar with a history of gaffes challenging Trump's own, Biden is a popular figure; he's got blue-collar appeal. But Biden is also an old white man, and the Democratic Party believes that President Obama's coalition can only be replicated by a member of an intersectional minority. Democrats also think that Clinton was too moderate for her own good — and so, now they're attempting to oust Sen. Dianne Feinstein, D-Calif., in favor of someone more radical. Thus Sens. Elizabeth Warren, Kamala Harris and Cory Booker.

Good luck, guys.

But Democrats have an even worse problem: their obvious disdain for Americans who didn't vote for them. Nowhere has that disdain been more evident than in their treatment of gun owners after the Parkland massacre. Democrats have cheered gun control advocates who question the decency of Second Amendment supporters. They have slandered legal gun owners as uncaring nasties more concerned with preserving pieces of metal than children's lives. They might as well call gun owners deplorables.

Good luck with that one, too.

The dirty little secret of 2016 is that President Trump didn't win the election — Clinton lost it. Democrats could easily do the same thing in 2020 if they insist that Americans must be taught a lesson for their 2016 heresy.

Intersectionality and Anti-Semitism

March 7, 2018

Nation of Islam leader Louis Farrakhan is an anti-Semite. This isn't in question. It's a fact, and one the minister continues to underscore with each speech. Last week, he spoke before the 2018 Saviours' Day event in Chicago. He stated: "White folks are going down. And Satan is going down. And Farrakhan, by God's grace, has pulled the cover off the eyes of that Satanic Jew, and I'm here to say your time is up, your world is through." Just for good measure, he added, "Jews were responsible for all of this filth and degenerate behavior that Hollywood is putting out," suggested that Jews are "the children of the devil" and claimed, "when you want something in this world, the Jew holds the door."

He's not a subtle fellow.

Which makes it utterly stunning that so many top-level Democrats have been able to get away with hobnobbing with him. Just weeks ago, we found out that Farrakhan met with the members of the Congressional Black Caucus in 2005, including then-Sen. Barack Obama; 21 current members of Congress were at that meeting. None of them have denounced Farrakhan. Rep. Danny Davis, D-Il., asked about Farrakhan on Sunday, stated, "I don't have no problems with Farrakhan. ... I know the Jews and Farrakhan ... The world is so much bigger than Farrakhan and the Jewish question and his position on that and so forth."

Tamika Mallory, one of the leaders of the Women's March on Washington, was personally present at Farrakhan's lecture in Chicago. Another Women's March leader, Carmen Perez, routinely touts Farrakhan on her social media. And anti-Semite Linda Sarsour spoke at a Nation of Islam event three years ago. All three have defended Farrakhan. Mallory took to Twitter to explain: "Jesus had a number of enemies as do all black leaders. Period point blank." Perez stated, "There are no perfect leaders." And Sarsour defended another anti-Semite from questions about Farrakhan.

Yet the mainstream media's attention to this odd spate of events has been relatively muted. Imagine, for a moment, that the House Freedom Caucus had met with former Ku Klux Klan leader David Duke. Imagine top tea party leaders had done so as well. Then imagine they had been questioned by members of the media about their associations and proceeded to dismiss such questions as irrelevant. Would we ever hear the end of the story? Of course not. President Trump is still living down his tacit nods at the "alt-right" during the 2016 campaign, as he should. But top Democrats openly embrace the anti-Semitism of Louis Farrakhan, and the only major media figure who seems to give a damn is CNN's Jake Tapper.

All of which demonstrates that where the media are concerned, intersectional identity matters far more than blatant bigotry. Farrakhan is black; the Congressional Black Caucus is, too; Mallory is black; Perez is Mexican-American; Sarsour is Muslim. This means that we're supposed to ignore their anti-Semitism. Were these characters all white Christian Republicans rather than minority Democrats, this would be front-page news each day.

The sin of intersectionality lies in the willingness of its devotees to discard virtue for identity politics. Anti-Semitism is anti-Semitism, no matter who purveys it. If only the members of the Democratic Party and the media felt the same way.

Until Democrats Come to Grips With Why Hillary Lost, Trump Will Keep Winning

March 14, 2018

Last weekend, Hillary Clinton spoke in India. There, she continued to struggle publicly with the most humiliating experience of her life, not her husband's continual sexual misconduct or her State Department's mishandling of Benghazi but her loss of the presidency to a reality television show host. Hillary's not over it. And she never will be.

That much was obvious from her incredible, palpable anger at the American public. She first explained that Trump voters are stupid poor people: "what the map doesn't show you is that I won the places that represent two-thirds of America's gross domestic product. So I won the places that are optimistic, diverse, dynamic, moving forward."

But Clinton wasn't done. She then stated that Trump voters are ignoramuses who still stumble out to their outhouses in the middle of the night and stoop over a hole in the ground while reading old copies of Ku Klux Klan newsletters. Those people, she said, fell prey to Trump's racist "Elmer Gantry" pitch: "you didn't like black people getting rights. You don't like women ... getting jobs. You don't want to ... see that Indian-American succeeding more than you are. Whatever your problem is, I'm going to solve it."

For good measure, Clinton tore into women who voted for Trump as well — and suggested that they are all little Tammy Wynettes standing by their men. "(W)e don't do well with married white women," Clinton explained. "And part of that is an identification with the Republican Party, and a sort of ongoing pressure to vote the way that your husband, your boss, your son, whoever believes you should." Yes, women who voted Republican only did so because they are afraid that ol' Bob is going to come home, get the beatin' stick out of the closet and start a-whoopin' and a-whalin' on the little woman.

And then, Democrats wonder why they had trouble winning Michigan, Pennsylvania and Wisconsin.

Here's the reality: None of this is true. The average Trump voter outearned the average Clinton voter, and 86 percent of Trump voters were employed, about the same percentage as Clinton voters. Tribalism in voting exists on both sides: The intersectional politics of the Democratic Party is inherently race based, and Trump successfully responded to that sort of politics in reactionary fashion. As to the notion that married women didn't vote for Clinton because of their husbands, 52 percent of married women voted for Trump; 53 percent of married women voted Republican candidate Mitt Romney in 2012, and 51 percent voted for Republican candidate John McCain in 2008. Married women vote differently than single women not because of pressure from their menfolk but because they often have children, value family over career more than single women and are older than single women on average.

But here's the point: Clinton represents a nasty, vengeful take on populations she has trouble winning over. That nastiness has filtered through the Democratic Party, which is firmly convinced that it'd be better off drilling down into population groups it thinks are interested in tearing down the system along with them than reaching out to populations it has lost. If Democrats continue with that quest, they'll alienate the very voters who gave Trump victory in 2016.

Stop Making Children Into Moral Authorities

March 21, 2018

On March 14, high school students from Parkland, Florida, led a school walkout in favor of gun control. The media have already appointed student witnesses of the horror at Marjory Stoneman Douglas High School untouchable moral authorities; their opinions are not to be questioned.

But now, the left has found even more sympathetic faces for its agenda: kindergarteners. According to The Wall Street Journal, "Schools are grappling with how to address the event with children as young as 5 years old and with finding ways for children who are too little to be told about school shootings to take part." Children in pre-K at Manhattan Country School will sing, "If I Had a Hammer" and "Paz y Libertad." Public schools like PS 321 in Brooklyn allowed children to do activities linked with the protests.

There is something deeply perverse about using children to promote a political agenda. Children simply don't know anything about politics. Sometimes children ask questions that help us rethink the world because they've had little experience with it — when my 4-year-old daughter asks questions about the universe, that prompts me to further learning and research. But she doesn't have *answers*, because she's a child.

What makes children particularly valuable is their innocence, not their ignorance. The left seems to like conflating the two characteristics. Innocence, as a quality, isn't about lack of knowledge or gullibility. The fact that everything in the world is wondrous to children is charming, but it's not something we can truly protect; as children age, they learn more, and they become more jaded, as we all do. We experience moments of wonder throughout our lives but never as we do when we're young. That's natural.

But we *can* protect innocence.

Innocence is the moral quality of being sinless, and children are inherently innocent specifically *because* they have not yet developed the ability to distinguish right from wrong. Once they do, the only way to maintain their innocence is for them to do right — the same way we all attempt to maintain our innocence.

But children must first be taught right from wrong. That means that as children develop their capacity to choose, they must develop a moral compass. Children don't have such a compass — the most selfish, cruel and nasty human beings on Earth are small children. If 2-year-olds had the capacity to carry weapons of war, we'd all be dead already; my son isn't yet 2 and takes a peculiar pleasure in knocking down his sister's blocks. That's why it's a good thing they're so damned cute.

But they're not moral guides. We must protect them from having to act as moral guides until they are prepared to do so. And that means we must stop using their innocence — their lack of capacity for moral decision-making — as a substitute for moral authority. To do anything less isn't merely foolish; it's cruel.

A New Kind of Gridlock

March 28, 2018

When the Founding Fathers wrote the Constitution of the United States, they feared the possibility of partisanship overtaking rights-based government. To that end, they crafted a system of checks and balances designed to pit interest against interest, promoting gridlock over radical change. The founders saw legislators, presidents and judges as ambitious in their pursuit of power.

They could not have foreseen our politicians.

Our politicians aren't so much ambitious for power as they are afraid of accountability. And so, we have a new sort of gridlock on Capitol Hill: Politicians campaign in cuttingly partisan fashion and then proceed to avoid solving just the sorts of issues on which they campaigned.

Last week, for example, Republicans passed a massive $1.3 trillion omnibus funding package to avert a government shutdown. It included full funding for Planned Parenthood and the regional Gateway rail project, but not full funding for the border wall. Republicans had spent years decrying deficits, criticizing funding for Planned Parenthood and ripping useless stimulus spending; they'd spent years clamoring for a border wall. When push came to shove, they did nothing.

Meanwhile, Democrats tore into the Republican budget for failing to ensure the permanent residence of so-called DREAMers, immigrants living in the United States illegally who were brought to the country as children. Then they rallied in Washington, D.C., along with gun control-minded students from Parkland, Florida, calling for more regulations on the Second Amendment. When Democrats held control of Congress and the presidency from 2009 to 2011, however, they promulgated no new gun legislation and passed no protection for DREAMers. Instead, then-President Barack Obama issued an executive action during his re-election cycle after saying repeatedly that he could not legally do so, and he complained incessantly about guns.

So, what should this tell us?

It should tell us that we, the voters, are suckers.

Our politicians use hot-button political issues in order to gin up the base and get us out to vote. They talk about how they'll end funding for Planned Parenthood and cut back spending on the right; they talk about how they'll end gun violence and protect DREAMers on the left. Then, once in power, they instead focus on broadly popular legislation instead of passing the legislation they've promised. They campaign for their base, but they govern for the center.

So, what are the *real* differences between the parties? The Republican Party is in favor of tax cuts and defense spending; the Democratic Party is in favor of increased regulation and social spending. All the other discussion points are designed merely to drive passion.

Practically speaking, this means gridlock on the issues about which Americans care most. Don't expect Republicans to stop funding Planned Parenthood anytime soon. And don't expect Democrats to start pushing serious gun control. They keep those issues alive deliberately to inflame excitement during election campaigns. Then, once in power, those issues go back into the freezer, to emerge and be defrosted when the time is right.

It's a convenient ploy. It means that partisan voters will never buck their party — after all, if the other side gets into power, they'll *really* go nuts. And, hey, maybe *this time*, our party bosses won't lie to us.

But they will. And we'll swallow it. And the government will grow. But at least we'll have the comfort slamming one another over issues that will never get solved.

The Grisly History of Chappaquiddick

April 4, 2018

On April 6, a bombshell will hit America's theaters.

That bombshell comes in the form of an understated, well-made, well-acted film called "Chappaquiddick." (Full disclosure: They advertise with my podcast.) The film tells the story of Ted Kennedy's 1969 killing of political aide Mary Jo Kopechne; the Massachusetts Democratic senator drove his car off a bridge and into the Poucha Pond, somehow escaped the overturned vehicle and left Kopechne to drown. She didn't drown, though. Instead, she reportedly suffocated while waiting for help inside an air bubble while Kennedy waited 10 hours to call for help. The Kennedy family and its associated political allies then worked to cover up the incident. In the end, Teddy was sentenced to a two-month suspended jail sentence for leaving the scene of an accident. The incident prevented Kennedy from running for president in 1972 and 1976, though he attempted a run in 1980 against then-President Jimmy Carter, failing.

So, why is the film important?

It's important because it doesn't traffic in rumors and innuendo — there is no attempt to claim that Kopechne was having an affair with Kennedy, or that she was pregnant with his child. It's important because it doesn't paint Kennedy as a monster but as a deeply flawed and somewhat pathetic scion of a dark and manipulative family. But most of all, it's important for two reasons: It's the first movie to actually tackle a serious Democratic scandal in the history of modern film, and it reminds us that Americans have long been willing to overlook scandal for the sake of political convenience.

First, there's the historic nature of the film. Here is an incomplete list of the films made about George W. Bush's administration since his election in 2000, nearly all of them accusatory in tone: "W," "Fahrenheit 9/11," "Recount," "Fair Game" and "Truth." There has still not been a movie made about former President Bill Clinton's impeachment (though one is apparently in the works). There's been no movie about former President Franklin Delano Roosevelt's internment of the Japanese, former President Lyndon Johnson's dramatic mishandling of the Vietnam War (though we have had two hagiographies of LBJ, one directed by Rob Reiner, the other starring Bryan Cranston) or former President Woodrow Wilson's racism and near fascism.

And it only took nearly 50 years to make a film about a Democratic icon leaving a woman to die in a river. It's amazing it was made in the first place.

Most importantly, though, "Chappaquiddick" reminds us that confirmation bias and wishful thinking aren't unique to one side of the aisle. In the era of President Trump, media members have had fun telling Republicans that they have abandoned all of their moral principles in order to back a man whose agenda they support. But Democrats beat Republicans there by decades: They not only overlooked a man who likely committed manslaughter but also made him into a hero, the "Lion of the Senate." We can't understand how morals and politics have been split in two without reckoning with this history.

"Chappaquiddick" is a must-see. It's just a shame it took half a century for it to see the light.

The Death of the DOJ and the FBI

April 11, 2018

This week, the FBI raided the office, hotel room and home of President Trump's personal attorney and self-described "fixer," Michael Cohen. According to various media reports, the Department of Justice signed off on a warrant for the search; presumably, the law enforcement agency is searching for evidence regarding Cohen's $130,000 payment to pornography actress Stormy Daniels, who allegedly had a one-night stand with Trump in 2006. Cohen has openly stated that he paid Daniels to shut up about her peccadillo with Trump — and he has said that Trump had no knowledge of the payment.

That presents a problem. If Cohen paid off Daniels without Trump's knowledge, that raises the question as to whether their agreement was binding. If not, then Trump may have been party to a violation of campaign finance law, since a $130,000 in-kind donation is well above any legal limit. And if Cohen and Trump coordinated that arrangement, none of their communications on the matter are subject to attorney-client privilege.

So, it's quite possible that the FBI and DOJ may have just ensnared Cohen and, by extension, Trump, in a serious scandal.

But this raises another question: Where the hell were the FBI and DOJ when it came to Hillary Clinton? Trump himself has been enraged by the disparity between law enforcement's treatment of Clinton and its treatment of him. He rightly points out that the FBI and DOJ worked to exonerate Clinton, with former FBI Director James Comey going so far as to change the definition of existing law to avoid recommending her indictment for mishandling classified material. And not only did then-Attorney General Loretta Lynch meet with former President Bill Clinton on a tarmac in the middle of the election cycle and the investigation of his wife; Lynch's Department of Justice allowed Cheryl Mills, Hillary Clinton's top aide, to claim attorney-client privilege. As Andrew McCarthy of National Review pointed out at the time, Mills was involved in the scrubbing of over 30,000 emails, yet the DOJ "indulged her attorney-client privilege claim, which frustrated the FBI's ability to question her on a key aspect of the investigation." Furthermore, Mills was allowed to sit in on Clinton's interview with the FBI as Clinton's lawyer.

And herein lies the problem for the DOJ and the FBI. Let's assume, for a moment, that everything they're doing now is totally honest and aboveboard — that there's no attempt to "get" President Trump and they're just following where the evidence leads. Many conservatives will *rightly* point to the DOJ and FBI treatment of Hillary Clinton, and state that the agencies ought to be consistent in their application of the law and leave Trump alone. Or they'll suggest that Trump ought to turn those agencies into personal defense organizations, as former President Obama did.

Once supposedly neutral organizations are made partisan, a return to neutrality *looks* partisan. That means that the FBI and DOJ damn well better have gold-plated evidence against Cohen; they better not leak ancillary information damaging Trump to the press; and they better have dotted all their i's and crossed all their t's. If not, there will be hell to pay, not merely for those agencies but for a country that can no longer trust its own law enforcement agencies.

If You Don't Agree With Me, You're a Racist Who Likes Death Threats

April 18, 2018

On Monday, George Yancy, a black professor of philosophy at Emory University, wrote a lengthy piece in The New York Times detailing the awful death threats he has received from white racists. I can sympathize — throughout 2016, I received my fair share of death threats. But Yancy sees those death threats as representative of a deeper malignancy plaguing all of white America, not a sickness within a subset of the population. Thus, he asks, "Should I Give up on White People?"

Yancy's case isn't particularly strong.

According to him, he faces a serious dilemma: "Do I give up on white people, on white America, or do I continue to fight for a better white America, despite the fact that my efforts continue to lead to forms of unspeakable white racist backlash?" But why exactly is that a serious dilemma? America isn't filled with racists — America is one of the least racist places on Earth, and its rate of racism has been decreasing steadily for years. In order for Yates' complaint to make any sense, he has to believe that America is actually becoming *more* racist.

And he does. He says that he is "convinced that America suffers from a pervasively malignant and malicious systemic illness — white racism." He offers no statistics to support this contention. And he suggests that those who disagree with his contention do so out of willingness to ignore white racism: "There is also an appalling lack of courage, weakness of will, spinelessness and indifference in our country that helps to sustain it."

So, to get this straight, you may not be racist, but if you believe that most Americans aren't racist, just like you, you're an aider and abettor of racism. You're in league with those sending the death threats. In fact, you're a monster under almost any circumstances. Yancy calls white Americans "monsters ... Land takers. Brutal dispossession. And then body snatchers and the selling and buying of black flesh." No one alive in the United States has forcibly dispossessed anyone of land; this has been true for generations. No one alive in the United States has been involved in the slave trade. Yet the legacy of white racism lives on in us, according to Yancy.

So, how are white Americans to escape this label?

Only by agreeing with Yancy. He praises one of his white students who agreed: "The system is racist. As a white woman, I am responsible to dismantle that system as well as the attitudes in me that growing up in the system created. I am responsible for speaking out when I hear racist comments."

Well, of course we're responsible for speaking out when we hear racist comments. That's not a revelation. But Yancy wants more than that. He wants a collective oath by white people to never deny generalized white racism, fact-free or not.

Which, of course, is racist. Yes, racism plays a central role in American history. Yes, there are still racists in America. But slandering white America in general for the crimes of a few bad apples is no better than slandering black America for the crimes of a few. If Yancy wants to deal with racist death threats, he could start by recognizing that we're all in this together — and that we side with him against those who threaten him — rather than pre-emptively characterizing us as the types of people who would write such vitriolic and evil screeds.

Who Controls Your Kids' Lives?

April 25, 2018

Former Republican Sen. Phil Gramm of Texas was fond of telling a story about his time stumping for educational change. "My educational policies are based on the fact that I care more about my children than you do," Gramm once said to a woman. "No, you don't," she replied. "OK," said Gramm. "What are their names?"

Gramm's fundamental premise is inalterably correct: Parents care more about their children than do the members of the bureaucracy. But parents are being gradually curbed in their authority by precisely those bureaucrats across the West.

On Tuesday, a British court condemned a not-yet-2-year-old child to die. Now, make no mistake: The child, Alfie Evans, is expected to die in the near future anyway; he suffers from an undiagnosed brain condition that has robbed him of much of his function. But his parents simply wanted to be able to transfer him from a British hospital to an Italian hospital to seek experimental care.

And the British court system refused.

Citing the expertise of Evans' doctors, the courts declared that Evans' best interests are not served by his parents' attempts to save his life. Instead, the little boy would be deprived of life support, left to die without oxygen or water. The ruling, the judge said, "represents the final chapter in the life of this extraordinary little boy." But that chapter was written by the British bureaucracy, not by his parents — the ones who will have to engrave his epitaph and visit his grave.

This appalling result isn't the first of its kind; just last year, a little boy named Charlie Gard was taken off life support thanks to the British court system, which presented his parents from sending him to the United States for further treatment. Again, the courts made the argument that the best interest of the child lay in his death.

All of this is the final result of a system of thought that places parental control of children below the expertise of bureaucrats on the scale of priorities. It's one thing for the government to step in when parents are preventing children from receiving life-saving care. It's another when the government steps in to prevent parents from *pursuing* potentially life-saving care. And yet that's just what has happened repeatedly in the United Kingdom.

Why? Why would British society place parents' wishes below the wishes of the state? Because a bureaucratic society of experts generally sees parents as an obstacle to proper development. Parents, in this view, treat their children as chattel to be owned and trained — but the state can treat children with the dignity they are due. This means placing parental wishes to the side in every case in which those wishes come into conflict with the priorities of the state.

The bureaucrats of Britain don't merely usurp parental rights in the realm of life and death; they do so in the realm of upbringing as well. They have threatened religious Jewish schools for failing to inculcate children with LGBT propaganda; meanwhile, they have ignored the targeting of young women in Rotherham, Rochdale, Oxford and Newcastle because the perpetrators are disproportionately Muslim.

All of this is untenable, both morally and practically. Parents will not continue to give the power to control their children away to bureaucrats who do not know their children's names.

Oh, Say Kanye Sees

May 2, 2018

It's easy to dismiss Kanye West.

It's easy to dismiss him because he's nutty. This is a fellow who tweets about antique fish tanks and fur pillows. This is the guy who calls himself Yeezus (after Jesus) and suggested that then-President George W. Bush didn't care about black people in the aftermath of Hurricane Katrina. He isn't exactly known for his bouts of emotional stability.

And in our celebrity-driven culture, we shouldn't pay too much attention to those who haven't spent a lot of time studying policy. That's how we end up with celebrity politicians, emotion-driven policy and reality television substituting for news.

With that said, Kanye West did something deeply important over the last two weeks: He opened up the debate.

Stung by the gratuitous censorship of the left, West began tweeting that Americans ought to think for themselves. He even tweeted a picture of himself wearing a "Make America Great Again" hat. And suddenly, the left went nuts, too. Kumail Nanjiani, co-writer of "The Big Sick," tweeted, "This was the worst twitter day in twitter history." Op-eds ran at The Root and The Washington Post claiming that West had been suckered.

But surprisingly, West didn't back down. He soon released a track with fellow rapper T.I. debating the merits of coming out as pro-Trump, with T.I. tearing into him as out of touch and West defending himself as thinking outside "the plantation." West met with conservative activist Candace Owens and tweeted quotes from Thomas Sowell.

Now, none of this means that West should suddenly be considered for leadership of The Heritage Foundation. But it does mark a break in the solid leftist wall of Hollywood and the music industry, and in the intersectional coalition.

The entertainment industry can't tolerate conservatives — when I wrote a book on political bias in Hollywood, several Hollywood insiders told me openly that they refuse to hire those on the right. Shania Twain learned just a few weeks ago that signaling support for President Trump in any way means taking your career into your hands.

The same holds true in identity politics circles. Those on the left who suggest that politics must innately follow immutable biological characteristics (i.e. black people have to be Democrats) felt deeply threatened by West's comments. After Chance the Rapper tweeted out that black Americans don't have to vote Democrat, the left's pressure snapped into place so rigidly that he backed off and apologized.

But West hasn't.

What's happening? It's doubtful that West started reading Edmund Burke. It may just be that West, like a lot of Americans tired of being told what to think by their industry and racialists on all sides, is getting tired of being told what to do. It's possible that West, like most Americans, sees America as a place with problems but a place where individuals can think and achieve freely. And he's clearly willing to take part in a political debate so many of his friends aren't.

That makes West an important voice, at least for now. It does take courage to buck your entire cadre in order to publicly declare what you think. West deserves credit for that. And who knows? Perhaps some other prominent Americans might come forward to re-engage in a debate from which they have been barred.

The Day the Iran Deal Died

May 9, 2018

Team Obama lives in a world of fiction.

As President Trump announced to the world that he would finally put a stake through the heart of the Iran deal — the signal foreign policy "achievement" of the Obama administration — Obama's former staffers lamented, rending their sackcloth and smearing their ashes. "I will never forget the dark cloud that hung over the White House in the years Iran was advancing nuclear program & Obama was briefed on all the risks of using military force," former United Nations Ambassador Samantha Power tweeted. "Trump has demolished America's credibility & paved the way for Iran to re-start its nuclear program. Trump has done the unthinkable: isolated the US & rallied the world around Iran."

Then there was amateur-fiction-writer-turned-professional-fiction-writer Ben Rhodes, a former Obama national security aide, who tweeted, "One tragicomic element of Trump's presidency is that the more he tries to tear down Obama's legacy, the bigger he makes Obama look." Meanwhile, former Secretary of State John Kerry, who had been traveling the world in an attempt to conduct his own personal foreign policy on behalf of the mullahs, stated, "Today's announcement weakens our security, breaks America's word, isolates us from our European allies, puts Israel at greater risk, empowers Iran's hardliners, and reduces our global leverage to address Tehran's misbehavior."

Obama himself stated, "Walking away from the JCPOA turns our back on America's closest allies."

In hearing all of these honeyed voices speak, one might think that Iran has been acting responsibly for the last three years, that it hasn't been pursuing a campaign of horrific terrorism in Yemen and Syria, that it hasn't been sponsoring the takeover of Lebanon by the terrorist group Hezbollah, that it hasn't been funding the Palestinian terror group Hamas, that it hasn't been developing long-range ballistic missiles while leading chants saying "Death to America." One might think that Obama left the Middle East a bright a beautiful place, not a hellhole filled with human carnage bought with dollars spent by Iran but funneled through the United States.

None of that is true, of course. Obama left the Middle East a smoking wreckage heap — a situation so grim that even Saudi Arabia, Egypt and Jordan have been forced to ally with Israel to allay fears of an Iranian regional takeover. Obama and his staff lied repeatedly to the American people about the Iran deal — and they continue to lie. When Kerry says that the deal will "empower Iran's hardliners," he is repeating an outright fabrication: The hardliners are in charge of the government, and the deal strengthened them. When Power speaks as though Obama alleviated the possibility of Iran's nuclear program, she's lying, too: The deal explicitly paved the way for an Iranian nuclear program free and clear of consequences from the international order. When Obama speaks as though our Middle East allies were pleased by the deal, he's lying: They all opposed it, and they're all celebrating its end.

Barack Obama had a peculiar vision of the Middle East remade: Iran ascendant, the power of Israel checked, the Saudis chastened. He achieved that vision at the cost of tens of thousands of lives across the region. President Trump is undoing that legacy. Good riddance.

Why Jerusalem Matters

May 16, 2018

This week, the Trump administration inaugurated the new American embassy in Jerusalem. The celebration in Israel was palpable; the embassy move came amidst the national celebration of the 70th anniversary of the creation of the state. The streets filled with Jews of all sorts, cheering and dancing.

Meanwhile, on the Gaza border, Hamas broadened its monthlong campaign to break down the Israel border, staging border "protests" attended by thousands — including terrorists who have used the supposed protests as a staging point for violent attacks on Israeli troops and territory. Palestinian terrorists have caused mass chaos, throwing Molotov cocktails at troops, attempting to rush the border, flinging explosives and tying incendiaries to kites in an attempt to set Israeli territory alight. The Israeli Defense Forces have responded with restraint. Despite this, a few dozen Palestinians have been killed, not the hundreds or thousands Hamas would presumably prefer.

But even as Yahya Sinwar, leader of Hamas in Gaza, suggested that "more than 100,000 people could storm the fence" between Israel and Gaza, and as 23-year-old Mohammed Mansoura announced, "We are excited to storm and get inside ... to kill, throw stones," the media covered the slow-rolling terror assault as a form of peaceful protest. A New York Times headline read "Israeli Troops Kill Dozens of Palestinian Protesters." A Wall Street Journal headline reads "Scores Killed, Thousands Injured as Palestinians Protest US Embassy Opening In Jerusalem."

Never mind that the riots had been going on for weeks preceding the embassy opening. Never mind that Hamas and the Palestinian

Authority could quickly and permanently end all violence simply by stopping the violence. The real issue, according to the press, is President Trump and his Israeli friends.

What drives the leftist press's coverage? Simply put, antipathy to the West. Israel is seen as an outpost of colonialism by leftists, and has been since the 1967 war. Then-President Barack Obama expressed the view well in his 2009 speech in Cairo, suggesting that Israel's rationale relied on its "tragic history" that "culminated in an unprecedented Holocaust." In this view, the Palestinians were shunted aside in favor of providing national reparations to Jews; the Jews took their Western ways into the heart of a foreign region.

This isn't true. The living proof of that is Israel's eternal connection to Jerusalem. That's why both radical Muslims (including the Palestinian leadership) and the far left deny Israel's historic bond with its homeland and hope desperately to stop public recognition of that bond. If Israel exists because Jewish connection pre-existed everything else, then Israel isn't a new outpost of the West; it's the oldest center of the West. That's why Trump's announcement is important: It's a recognition that the West was founded on Jerusalem, rather than the other way around.

Peace will come when everyone recognizes what Trump has recognized: The Jewish connection to Jerusalem is unbreakable. And peace will come when Israel's enemies realize that violence can't change that underlying fact.

How the Russia Investigation Helps Trump

May 23, 2018

This week, for the first time in months, a generic ballot poll showed Republicans beating Democrats in the midterm elections. According to Reuters, Republicans are now leading by six points. And while that poll is obviously an outlier, the movement of the generic ballot in the direction of Republicans isn't: The average lead for Democrats has been dropping steadily since late February, from a nine-point lead to a four-point lead.

Why?

Certainly, the economy has something to do with it: The job market continues to boom; the stock market continues to hover around 25,000; and GDP continues to grow steadily. And, certainly, foreign policy has something to do with it: There are no catastrophic foreign wars on the horizon, and President Trump's gutsy calls to pull out of the Iran nuclear deal and move the U.S. embassy in Israel to Jerusalem resulted in zero serious backlash.

Democrats opposed the Trump tax cuts and have whined incessantly about Trump's Middle East foreign policy, even going so far as to demonstrate a certain level of warmth toward terrorist group Hamas. This isn't exactly brilliant politicking.

But there's another reason Democrats seem to be dropping like a stone, too: their Russia obsession. The reality is most Americans think the Russia investigation is going nowhere. As of early May, just 44 percent of Americans though the FBI special counsel investigation of President Trump and his associates is justified; fifty-three percent thought that the investigation is politically motivated. Three-quarters of Americans think Trump should cooperate with the probe, but Americans are skeptical that there is a *there* there.

And so far, Americans have been right. Special counsel Robert Mueller's investigation has resulted in indictments of Trump associates on a charge of lying to the FBI, but there have been no indictments related to the original brief of his investigation: election collusion with the Russians. Meanwhile, each day seems to bring new headlines regarding the extent of the FBI investigation, dating all the way back to mid-2016. Americans aren't going to read all the details of the various stories — they're just going to take away that law enforcement was all over the Trump campaign, has come up with nothing thus far and continues to hound the Trump White House.

Furthermore, Democrats are getting discouraged. They were promised a *deus ex machina* — an alien force that would swoop in to end the Trump presidency. They hoped it would be Mueller; they were convinced the election was stolen. It wasn't, and it's unlikely Mueller will end Trump's presidency.

So when Trump fulminates about the supposed sins of the "deep state," few Americans are exercised. Most shrug; some even nod along. Democrats seethe but have no new fodder for their ire — and every day that passes with the media chumming the waters and coming up empty drives down enthusiasm even more. And Trump's focus on Russia means that he spends less time tweeting about other topics — which helps him, since he's less likely to make a grave error on those fronts.

If Mueller truly has nothing, there's a serious case to be made that the Russia collusion investigation actually *helped* Trump more than it hurt him. And Democrats might just have to come up with a plan for dealing with Trump's policies other than praying for an avenging angel to frog-march him from the White House.

The Suicide of Europe

May 30, 2018

On Friday, the British police arrested Tommy Robinson, founder and former leader of the English Defence League, a far-right anti-Islam group. Robinson is a controversial character, to be sure, a sort of Milo Yiannopoulos lite. His chief focus is on the threat of radical Islam, which he believes threatens the integrity of the British system.

You don't have to like Robinson. But whatever you think of him, his arrest is absurd by any measure. You see, Robinson was arrested for standing outside a court building and reporting on a trial involving the alleged grooming of young girls for sexual assault by radical Muslims.

Now, what would be illegal about that, you ask? It turns out that Robinson was given a suspended sentence last year for filming outside another court building, where a trial for alleged gang rape by radical Muslims was taking place. He wasn't inside the courtroom. Nonetheless, the judge believed he was somehow biasing the jurors. According to the judge, Robinson was sentenced thanks to "pejorative language which prejudges the case, and it is language and reporting ... that could have had the effect of substantially derailing the trial."

This time, Robinson was again arrested for prejudicing a case, only he wasn't inside the court building. He was outside. And the media were originally banned from reporting on his arrest so that *his* trial wouldn't be biased. In other words, Britain has now effectively banned reporting that actually mentions the Islamic nature of criminal defendants for fear of stirring up bigotry — and has banned reporting on reporting on such defendants. It's an infinite regress of suicidal political correctness.

But at least the Europeans have their priorities straight: While it's perfectly legal to lock up a provocateur covering a trial involving Muslims, the European Union is now considering a ban on products like cotton buds, straws and other plastics for fear of marine litter. And just as importantly, it's now perfectly legal to kill unborn children again in Ireland, where voters — with the help of a cheering press — decided to lift the ban on abortions until the 20th week, condemning thousands of children to death.

This is how the West dies: with a tut-tut, not with a bang. The same civilization that sees it as a fundamental right to kill a child in the womb thinks it is utterly out of bounds to film outside a trial involving the abuse of children, so long as the defendants are radical Muslims. The Europeans have elevated the right to not be offended above the right to life; they've elevated the right to not be offended above the right to free speech, all in the name of some utopian vision of a society without standards.

Discarding those standards was supposed to make Europeans more free; it was supposed to allow Europeans to feel more comfortable. But the sad truth is that *no* society exists without certain standards and Europe has a new standard: enforcement of its "tolerance" via jail sentence, combined with tolerance of multiculturalism that sees tolerance itself as a Trojan horse. The notion of individual rights sprang from European soil. Now they're beginning to die there.

Supreme Court: Be Polite When You Violate Others' Rights

June 6, 2018

This week, the Supreme Court ruled on the Masterpiece Cakeshop case. That case involved a religious Christian man, Jack Phillips, who decorates cakes for a living. Two men came into his shop one day and demanded that Phillips decorate a cake for their same-sex wedding. Phillips refused. For this grave breach of civic duty, the Colorado Civil Rights Commission referred his case for prosecution, ruling that he had breached the customers' rights to receive service.

The Supreme Court ignored the key issues of the case. It refused to countenance whether First Amendment speech rights could be violated in favor of nondiscrimination laws — whether, for example, a gay songwriter could be forced to perform work for an evangelical Christian choir looking for a tune to liven up Leviticus 18. It refused to consider whether First Amendment free association rights could be completely overthrown by reference to nondiscrimination laws — whether any business could be told to serve anyone for any reason at any time. Finally, it refused to consider whether First Amendment freedom of religion could be overturned in favor of nondiscrimination law — whether religious practice stops at the front door of the home and the church.

Instead, the court ruled that the baker didn't have to bake the cake because the members of the Colorado Civil Rights Commission were unduly mean. You see, the commission pilloried the man's religious viewpoint rather than giving it a respectful hearing; it compared his viewpoint to pro-slavery and pro-Holocaust viewpoints. This was extreme and nasty. Thus, Justice Anthony

Kennedy concluded: "The commission's hostility was inconsistent with the First Amendment's guarantee that our laws be applied in a manner that is neutral toward religion. ... The outcome of cases like this in other circumstances must await further elaboration in the courts."

I must have missed the "be kind; rewind" section of the First Amendment.

Of course, the Supreme Court likely ruled on narrow grounds in order to achieve a 7-2 majority including liberal Justices Elena Kagan and Stephen Breyer. But the ruling bodes ill for the future: It doesn't protect religious Americans, nor does it protect freedom of speech.

In reality, the founders would have been aghast at this issue ever rising to the level of the judiciary. Freedom of speech, and, by extension, freedom of association, were designed to allow private individuals to live their lives as they see fit, free of the burden of an overreaching government. Freedom of religion was to be guaranteed by a small government unconcerned with the day-to-day matters of business. Free markets were considered enough incentive to prevent mass discrimination in public accommodations.

Now, however, the courts have decided that the government can tell you what to say, who to say it to and how to act out your religion. The only holdup is that they have to be nice about telling you what to do.

Trump's Triumph or Kim's Coup?

June 13, 2018

This week, President Trump went to Singapore to meet with the most repressive dictator on the planet, North Korean Supreme Leader Kim Jung Un. Kim presides over a slave state of 25 million people, with gulags stacked with hundreds of thousands of political dissidents. He has diligently pursued nuclear weapons and long-range missile tests. He was greeted as a celebrity in Singapore, with President Trump shaking his hand, calling him "very smart" and "a funny guy" and generally praising him to the skies.

Fans of President Trump were ecstatic. To them, this was a breakthrough movement: an American leader sitting down with a North Korean leader, finally breaking through the clutter of the past to get down to brass tacks. To Trump critics, this was a debacle: The president handed Kim an unprecedented propaganda coup, complete with grinning photos and thumbs up before a backdrop of interpolated North Korean and American flags.

Here's the truth: We don't know what this will be yet. If it turns out that Trump has a trick up his sleeve — if it turns out that Trump has indeed convinced Kim to denuclearize and liberalize his country — then this will go down in history as a move of extraordinary genius. If, however, it's a photo op designed to allow Trump to claim status as a diplomatic wizard, and if Kim gives up nothing while the United States legitimizes an evil tyrant and ratchets down military exercises with South Korea, it will be a debacle.

This was a high-risk, high-reward strategy.

But it doesn't appear that the White House thinks of it that way. Instead, it seems to view the summit as an unalloyed win for President Trump no matter what happens next. Trump, they say, can always reverse himself. Trump himself made the same point: "Honestly, I think he's going to do these things. I may be wrong. ... I don't know that I'll ever admit that, but I'll find some kind of an excuse."

And herein lies the problem. Trump has a stake in *not being wrong*. That's why presidents typically don't hold face-to-face get-togethers with evil dictators until some sort of serious negotiation has already taken place. Trump is now invested in the success of his diplomacy, rather than in the strongest possible outcome alone. That's a win for Kim, at the very least. Trump has given Kim an advance against the possibility of future concessions. If those concessions never materialize, Trump will be forced to choose between admitting he was bamboozled and brazening through the humiliation, pretending that Kim is in fact a moderate force willing to work with him.

Right now, barring additional evidence of North Korean surrender, Kim has the upper hand. That could always change tomorrow; we should hope and pray that it will. If it doesn't, then President Trump not only won't get a win out of the North Korean summit; he'll have been played by a tin-pot dictator with a penchant for murdering his family members.

The Banality of Bias

June 20, 2018

Peter Strzok is an FBI agent with a career spanning more than two decades. He was section chief of the counterespionage section in 2016 and thus in a position to oversee both the Hillary Clinton email investigation and the Russian election interference investigation. And he was supposedly perfect for the job: a Georgetown University graduate with a master's degree, married to a Securities and Exchange Commission official. Strzok was qualified and patriotic. He was a lifelong civil servant.

He was also a heavily biased, blatantly political bureaucrat.

Strzok, it turns out, was cheating on his wife with then-fellow FBI agent Lisa Page. Page and Strzok traded thousands of texts — so many that one is tempted to ask when they ever found time for their affair. The texts were extraordinarily political. Strzok hated President Trump and loved Clinton; his paramour felt the same. After the 2016 election, Strzok wrote, "Omg I am so depressed." Among those texts, a few stood out. First, one from Strzok to Page suggested that the Russia investigation could serve as an "insurance policy" against a Trump presidency. Second, in a text from Page to Strzok, she questions whether Trump would actually be president, and a response from Strzok reads, "We'll stop it." Third, a text from Strzok to Page after the election cycle and upon his involvement in the Robert Mueller probe reads, "For me, and this case, I personally have a sense of unfinished business."

All of these texts — and Strzok's conduct during the election cycle — led the Department of Justice inspector general to conclude that he couldn't exonerate Strzok from the charge of bias in his investigation. The IG report stated that Strzok's texts were "not only indicative of a biased state of mind but, even more seriously, implies a willingness to take official action to impact the presidential candidate's electoral prospects. This is antithetical to the core values of the FBI and the Department of Justice."

Here's the thing: Strzok wasn't alone. At least four other FBI agents sent pro-Clinton messages throughout the Clinton investigation. One agent stated that nobody would prosecute Hillary Clinton "even if we find unique classified" material on former Rep. Anthony Weiner's laptop. Another texted, "Vive le resistance" after the election. And the IG report subtly slip in this rather shocking revelation: "We identified numerous FBI employees, at all levels of the organization and with no official reason to be in contact with the media, who were nevertheless in frequent contact with reporters." That contact included employees receiving "benefits from reports," such as golf outings, drinks and meals.

This is how bureaucratic agencies lose legitimacy: not with overt acts of evil but through the echo-chamber mentality that exists in every social setting. We all live within cliques; we all deal with a select group of people. If that select group of people thinks alike, the group tends to radicalize over time. And if there are no checks in place — if that clique has enormous power — it's easy to see how cases can get botched.

This is the problem with unelected, unaccountable, nontransparent bureaucracies: They are subject to ideological perversion that they themselves may not even notice until it is too late. That's why they should be extraordinarily careful in how they wield power. Unfortunately, our law enforcement agencies aren't, and the result is a dramatic loss of trust that they can ill afford.

The Rise of the Mob

June 27, 2018

This week, Rep. Maxine Waters, D-Calif., issued a clarion call to Democrats outraged at the policies of the Trump administration: It's time for mob action. In the wake of mobs targeting Secretary of Homeland Security Kirstjen Nielsen and Florida Attorney General Pam Bondi, Waters explained: "God is on our side! On the side of the children ... Let's make sure we show up wherever we have to show up. And if you see anybody from that Cabinet in a restaurant, in a department store, at a gasoline station, you get out and you create a crowd and you push back on them and you tell them they're not welcome anymore, anywhere."

Waters has always been a fan of mob action. She infamously touted the violent and brutal 1992 Los Angeles riots, which did approximately $1 billion in property damage and ended with 63 people dead. Waters called the events a "rebellion," labeling them a "spontaneous reaction to a lot of injustice and a lot of alienation and frustration." And yet Waters has been affectionately nicknamed "Auntie Maxine" thanks to her rabid attacks against the Trump administration.

Democratic leaders ranging from House Minority Leader Nancy Pelosi, D-Calif., to Senate Minority Leader Chuck Schumer, D-N.Y., denounced Waters' words. They've done the same with regard to violent protests on college campuses. That is meritorious and deserves praise.

But there is little question that major political figures on both sides of the aisle have played footsie with mob action to little or no blowback. It's not just Waters. President Obama made excuses for riots in Ferguson, Missouri, and Baltimore, Maryland, during his presidency; Rev. Al Sharpton, who has actually been involved in precipitating mob violence, still gets to play peacemaker on national television; during President Trump's 2016 campaign, he repeatedly referenced the possibility of violence against protesters.

No civil society can humor such overtures to mob action and remain civil for long. The First Amendment protects Maxine Waters, of course, and it should. But Americans should be appalled by her words, rather than slightly titillated by them. And yet it seems that extreme rhetoric now earns a sort of badge of "coolness" that can't be matched by those calling for cooler heads. To call for civility now seems unwoke. No wonder Symone Sanders of CNN stated, "the folks calling for civility might need to check their privilege." To be angry is to be justified; not being angry enough is the greatest sin.

And that *is* dangerous. It's not that Americans will suddenly begin attacking one another in the streets. It's that large populations can be moved by small, extreme minorities. Nassim Nicholas Taleb writes in his new book, "Skin in the Game," about the phenomenon of "renormalization," whereby larger, more moderate groups appease small minorities simply to avoid certain costs. That can happen when reasonable people stop standing up to advocates for mobocracy, afraid that doing so will alienate their most vocal supporters.

Waters has always been a fringe figure. Perhaps she'll remain so. But there are no guarantees. And we shouldn't be sanguine about the prospects of quashing radical tribalism. It's not quite as easy as putting out a few tepid statements.

What the Courts Are for

July 4, 2018

Democrats are in a state of sheer panic.

They're panicking because last week, Justice Anthony Kennedy — a reliable vote in favor of certain leftist priorities including abortion and same-sex marriage — announced that he will step down from the Supreme Court, leaving President Trump a second selection. This apparently will lead to the end of a free America. According to Jeffrey Toobin of CNN, the remade Supreme Court will spell doom: "Abortion illegal; doctors prosecuted; gay people barred from restaurants, hotels, stores; African-Americans out of elite schools; gun control banned in 50 states; the end of regulatory state."

None of this is true, of course. It simply demonstrates the wild overreach to which the left has subjected the judicial branch to date.

The judicial branch was never meant to act as a superlegislature, using the verbiage of the Constitution in order to implement preferred policy prescriptions. In Federalist No. 78, Alexander Hamilton expressed the idea well: "The courts must declare the sense of the law; and if they should be disposed to exercise WILL instead of JUDGMENT, the consequence would equally be the substitution of their pleasure to that of the legislative body." Substituting will for judgment would make the case for utterly dissolving the judicial branch.

Yet according to the Democrats, the Supreme Court *should* exercise will instead of judgment. The role of the court, according to Justice Sonia Sotomayor, is to help expedite change in our society: "Our society would be strait-jacketed were not the courts, with the able assistance of the lawyers, constantly overhauling the law and adapting it to the realities of ever-changing social, industrial and political conditions." Justice Elena Kagan believes the same thing, which is why she constantly describes the Constitution as "abstract," leaving her room to interpret it as poetry rather than statute.

This is why Democrats celebrate obviously superlegal decisions like Roe v. Wade: There is no right to abortion in the Constitution, but they would prefer not to battle that issue out at the electoral level. The Supreme Court allows them to hand down their policy from the mountaintop without having to subject those policies to public scrutiny.

And *that* means that any reversal of such policy by a Supreme Court that actually reads the Constitution as it was written is a threat to Democratic hegemony. Were President Trump to appoint an originalist to the Supreme Court, Roe v. Wade would surely die, but that wouldn't make abortion illegal — the issue would have to be put before the American public. Affirmative action from state schools would end, but African-Americans wouldn't be barred from attending elite institutions — such a bar would remain illegal. Gays across the country would not suddenly find themselves barred from public restaurants — it's unlikely the Supreme Court would rule such action legal, and even if it were to do so, virtually no establishments across the country would start asking about sexual orientation at the door.

In the end, the Democrats' obsession with the Supreme Court says more about them than about the role of the court. It says that they don't believe their policies are popular enough to win the country over at the electoral level. If the judiciary should be returned to its role of ruling by judgment rather than will, the will of the people might be heard once again — and it wouldn't be friendly to Democrats. Democrats know it. Hence the panic.

When Abortion Becomes a Sacrament

July 11, 2018

This week, amid widespread Democratic tumult regarding the selection of a replacement for Supreme Court Justice Anthony Kennedy, alleged comedian Michelle Wolf paid tribute to the most important facet of American life: abortion. On her Netflix show on Sunday, Wolf dressed up in red, white and blue, and shrieked into the camera, "God bless abortions, and God bless America!" She explained: "Women, if you need an abortion, get one! If you want an abortion, get one! ... And women, don't forget: You have the power to give life and men will try to control that. Don't let them!"

Along with that inane outburst, she justified abortion itself. "Look," she stated, "access to abortion is good and important. Some people say abortion is killing a baby. It's not. It's stopping a baby from happening."

Well, some people say Michelle Wolf is killing comedy. She's not. She's stopping comedy from happening.

But more importantly, a ground shift has taken place in how Democrats think about abortion. Back in 2005, I wrote that the Democratic "safe, legal and rare" formulation regarding abortion was logically and morally untenable: If Democrats wanted abortion to be rare thanks to its inherent immorality, there was no reason for it to be legal. Democrats have finally come around: They're now "shouting" their abortions, proclaiming them from the rooftops, suggesting that there is a moral *good* achieved by abortion.

Thus, Lena Dunham said just two years ago, "I still haven't had an abortion, but I wish I had." Thus, Chelsea Handler, who has had two abortions, explained in the pages of Playboy, "I don't ever look back and think, 'God, I wish I'd had that baby.'" Her article was accompanied by a picture of a woman's hand with a raised middle finger with a pink bow around it; attached to the bow is a small card that reads, "It's an abortion!"

Yes, abortion is now a signifier that you refuse to be ruled by the patriarchy. Avoidance of pregnancy may be a wise life choice, according to third-wave feminists, preventing women from being sucked into the grinding maw of maternal life. But abortion is something even better: a signal that you just don't care about the system. The system demands that if you're pregnant with a child, you make your own concerns secondary; the system must be fought.

Gloria Steinem once remarked, "If men could get pregnant, abortion would be a sacrament." But modern-day feminists have determined that abortion *is* a sacrament specifically *because* women can get pregnant: Showing that control over your body even extends to the killing of your unborn child is a way of standing up against patriarchal concerns with women as the source of future generations.

For Michelle Wolf, abortion isn't just another decision. It's a giant middle finger to the moral establishment. And those who would fight abortion are desacralizing the mysterious holiness of a ritual that reinforces women's control. No wonder Wolf thinks God blesses abortion; abortion is her god.

What Is Democratic Socialism?

July 18, 2018

The new rising star of the Democratic Party is Alexandria Ocasio-Cortez. The 28-year-old former bartender doesn't know much about politics — this week, she bungled her way through an interview answer by referring to Israeli "occupation" of Palestine and citing her lack of expertise on the issue despite her international relations degree. But she's young; she's energetic; and she speaks in glowing terms about rights to housing, food, college and health care. She's a charter member of the Democratic Socialists of America, a group, we're informed by The New York Times' Michelle Goldberg, that is on the rise. "Its growth has exploded since the 2016 election," Goldberg reports, "from 7,000 members to more than 37,000."

What exactly is democratic socialism, and what distinguishes it from socialism plain and simple? Ocasio-Cortez doesn't know. When asked about it by Meghan McCain on "The View," she stated that there is a "huge difference" between the two notions but then concluded, "I believe that in a moral and wealthy America, in a moral and modern America, no person should be too poor to live in this country." Which doesn't explain the difference at all.

The difference is truly between socialism and social democracy. Socialism suggests state ownership and control of all major resources — and generally ends with the complete collapse and destruction of the productive population. Social democracy suggests redistribution of capitalistic gains — more like Denmark or Norway or Sweden. It's unclear where Ocasio-Cortez lies on this spectrum considering that the DSA openly acknowledges its desire to abolish capitalism.

But let's assume that what Ocasio-Cortez and Democrats want is actually just European-style social democracy. If that's the case, they're still misreading the tea leaves: The Nordic countries aren't thriving and healthy because they're socialist; they're thriving and healthy because they are small and homogenous. In fact, Nordic lifestyles means that Nordic life expectancy outclassed life expectancy in the United States before the Nordic states tried to grow government redistributionism radically. The left is fond of citing Norway and Sweden — even though both are now moving in a politically right-wing direction — but neglecting Switzerland, which is just as successful and far less socialistic.

Furthermore, generous welfare policies can only operate in small, homogenous countries because if you open the borders to such countries, immigrants flood in and then sink the boat. That's why voters in Europe have been consistently moving toward a more restrictionist view of immigration — particularly in that bastion of social democracy, Sweden.

Yet the democratic socialist dream never dies, even as it fades away in Europe. Democrats will continue to point toward the Nordic states and claim that utopia is a mere "free lunch" program away. But lunch is never free, as a former bartender should know.

The Policy of Unintended Consequences

July 25, 2018

One of the great lies of modern politics is that when a policy fails, it's because someone just didn't *care* enough. It's a nostrum repeated frequently: If President Trump were to only care more about immigrant children, he'd find a way to unite them with their parents; if Democrats were to only care more about the homeless, they'd find a way to clean up Los Angeles and Seattle; if Republicans were to only care more about the sick, they'd find a way to bring down insurance premiums.

In reality, most failures are simply the result of unintended consequences.

Take, for example, President Trump's tariff policy. Trump believes that "Tariffs are the greatest," according to one of his tweets this week. Not only are they the greatest; they prevent us from becoming the "'piggy bank' that's being robbed." Trump looks across the vast savannas of the United States and sees domestic businesses undercut by foreign competition, and his immediate thought is to help those businesses by taxing their foreign competitors.

Unfortunately, his policy has unintended consequences: It raises prices and causes retaliatory tariffs. So domestic consumers pay more for products; domestic producers have to pay more for the inputs they use to manufacture their own products; and foreign markets are closed to American exporters. All of this means that some of the businesses Trump seeks to help actually get hurt, which is why both Whirlpool and Harley-Davidson have downgraded their profit expectations in the wake of Trump's policy.

But Trump still wants to demonstrate that he *cares*. And so, he undertakes a Band-Aid policy: subsidies to agricultural concerns hurt by his tariffs. This week, the administration announced a Department of Agriculture $12 billion subsidy directed at farmers who can no longer competitively export product to foreign markets. "(I)nstead of offering welfare to farmers to solve a problem they themselves created, the administration should reverse course and end this incoherent policy," Sen. Bob Corker, R-Tenn., accurately summed up.

It's not just Trump.

Democrats routinely complain about the price of rent in major cities but then institute rent control and subsidized housing, driving up the cost of development. In order to deal with the rising costs of rent, they push for an increase in the minimum wage, which causes more unemployment. Then they tax the businesses they've already penalized in order to pay for the unemployed.

Or they push for lower educational costs and seek government subsidies to drive down college tuition. But in doing so, they create a base rate colleges can now charge, driving up those rates.

Or they push for better Medicare subsidies, creating new demand, which drives up prices.

This is the problem with government policy in general: It's a blunderbuss. Collateral damage from any broad-based policy is likely to far surpass the damage undergone by individuals in a free market system, which means we ought to tread carefully when it comes to making such policy.

But we won't. Instead, we'll just chalk up such failures to a lack of will or spirit, and demand more action — action that will fail. And then we'll repeat the cycle over and over, never suspecting that perhaps it's our good intentions that got us into trouble in the first place.

Being a Socialist Means Never Having to Say You're Sorry

August 1, 2018

"So, how are you planning to pay for that?"

This should be the first question asked about any political program. Unfortunately, it's not. And that's why Sen. Bernie Sanders, I-Vt., and congressional candidate Alexandria Ocasio-Cortez, D-N.Y., are thought leaders for their parties.

Take Sanders. He has been promoting his "Medicare for All" slogan for years. The left loves it. Among the top Democrats who have embraced this slogan are Sen. Cory Booker, D-N.J., Sen. Elizabeth Warren, D-Mass., Sen. Kamala Harris, D-Calif., and Sen. Jeff Merkley, D-Ore. Most of those senators want to run for president. So they understand that Sanders' bumper sticker policy is popular on its face.

There's only one problem: Nobody asked that first question. This week, Charles Blahous of the Mercatus Center at George Mason University released a study taking a look at the cost of Sanders' preferred program. The total: $32.6 trillion over 10 years. Over that same period, our *total* federal spending is projected at $56 trillion — and we're already racking up debt like there's no tomorrow on that budget. That means that we could double our taxes at every level and still not come close to covering Sanders' program.

Sanders responded to this unfortunate news by attacking the study, blaming the nefarious Koch brothers for sponsoring Blahous' basic math. There's only one problem: The Urban Institute, a left-leaning outlet, estimated the cost at $32 trillion. So this isn't a right-left problem. It's a basic math problem. Sanders doesn't understand basic math.

Or, more accurately, he doesn't care about it. And he's not alone. Ocasio-Cortez recently embarrassed herself on this same topic. When asked about how she would pay for her program of free Medicare for All, college tuition and housing, she explained that we could just raise the corporate tax rate to 28 percent and close some loopholes, and "that's $2 trillion right there." Which would pay for ... approximately seven months of Medicare for All. Then, Ocasio-Cortez explained that she'd find money by cutting the defense budget ($700 billion per year), which would *still* not cover Medicare for All. And she'd create a carbon tax, which could crush industry, leading to lesser tax revenue.

But Democrats aren't interested in who pays for things, because their ultimate solution is that *nobody pays for things*. Yes, really. According to Stephanie Kelton, professor of public policy and economics at Stony Brook University — and a Sanders 2016 advisor — we can simply pay for things by paying for things. She says the only limit on spending is inflation. Even Paul Krugman of The New York Times has called this idea foolhardy: Inflation is inevitable once people realize that the government is literally just printing money to spend it, and once people begin socking away cash in order to avoid the exorbitant taxes they're sure will come.

The good news for Democrats is that nobody asks the key question. Even Republicans don't, which is why they spend trillions of dollars of their own. And so long as nobody is asking the question, Sanders and Ocasio-Cortez will be the future of the country ... until we run out of money.

Is Collusion Criminal?

August 8, 2018

In the last two weeks, the Trump administration has begun to make a rather interesting legal argument: Collusion isn't criminal. President Trump's lawyer Rudy Giuliani made this argument on television; Trump repeated it on Twitter. But is it true?

Technically, collusion isn't a crime. There is no statutory definition of "collusion"; the closest we could come is "conspiracy." So let's be more specific: Would it be criminal activity if the Trump campaign solicited opposition research from the Russian government? The short answer: Not clearly, unless the campaign was also involved in underlying criminal activity, such as hacking the Democratic National Committee or the Hillary Clinton campaign. UCLA professor of law Eugene Volokh explained in the Washington Post last year that barring such activity, it seems violative of the First Amendment to prevent campaigns from talking with foreign citizens about opposition research on other candidates. After all, Clinton's team paid Fusion GPS to create an opposition-research dossier, much of the material provided by a foreign citizen, Christopher Steele. Even exchanging information with the Russian government wouldn't clearly violate the law, if Volokh is correct.

Now, this doesn't mean that the Trump campaign is in the clear. It just means that Trump's opponents will have to prove far more than they've proved so far.

All of which means that the slim hook on which the Democratic hopes of a Trump criminal charge are based grows even more tenuous. Now Democrats are banking on the possibility of an obstruction charge emerging against Trump: perhaps, they say, Trump has attempted to shut down special counsel Robert Mueller's investigation in some way. After all, he's constantly tweeting about the myriad evils of the so-called "witch hunt." But even here, the statutory basis for such a charge is thin: There are provisions covering destruction of evidence or threatening to influence a "pending judicial proceeding," but obstruction generally requires an active attempt to impede — and the Mueller investigation, according to the testimony of Deputy Attorney General Rod Rosenstein, hasn't actually been impacted by Trump's fulmination.

The best hope for Democrats is a perjury charge against Donald Trump Jr. They hope that Trump Jr. lied when he said that his father didn't know about the June 2016 Trump Tower meeting with Russian lawyer Natalia Veselnitskaya; perhaps, they think, they can charge Trump Jr. with something to get him to flip on his father. But so far, there's been no evidence that Trump knew about that meeting, and Trump continues to deny it.

More and more, the Democratic hope for a deus ex machina to oust Trump seems like a chimerical fancy. (Even if Trump were to be indicted for a crime, it's utterly unclear constitutionally whether he could be prosecuted; the constitutional remedy for high crimes and misdemeanors is impeachment.) But they do have one hope yet: Trump could continue to pour out his feelings on Twitter, creating possible legal problems for himself and undermining his credibility with the American people.

That's why Trump should stop chatting about these matters. The more he chats, the higher the chances he creates a thicket he cannot escape. The Democrats' best hope at this point isn't the law or even Robert Mueller. It's President Trump's rage, and his pathological inability to avoid venting it in public fora.

What If Everybody Sucks at Everything?

August 15, 2018

This week, President Trump went on a Twitter rampage — rightly so — over the firing of FBI agent Peter Strzok. Strzok, you'll recall, is the agent who was tasked with overseeing both the Hillary Clinton email investigation and the Russian election-interference investigation. The married agent was texting with his married paramour, Lisa Page, at the time — and among their sexy texts was a bevy concerning their hatred for then-candidate Donald Trump. The Department of Justice inspector general report condemned Strzok's behavior, stating that it was "not only indicative of a biased state of mind but, even more seriously, implies a willingness to take official action to impact the presidential candidate's electoral prospect."

The only mystery is why Strzok's firing took so long.

Now, the common theory growing on the right is that Strzok, along with his like-minded allies in our nation's intelligence agencies, crafted a plot to stop the Trump campaign or oust Trump after his election. They cite Strzok's texts as evidence of motive, which it clearly is. They also cite the relationship between Fusion GPS, the opposition-research firm hired by Hillary Clinton, and Department of Justice employee Bruce Ohr, whose wife worked for Fusion GPS; the use of the so-called Steele dossier, funded by Fusion GPS, in the application for a Foreign Intelligence Surveillance Act warrant against former Trump campaign aide Carter Page; and the fact that Strzok maintained his employment with the FBI until now.

None of these accusations should be taken lightly. But there's another explanation that bears up under weight: Everybody sucks at everything. So, yes, Strzok was biased. But it's just possible that the

FBI initiated the Russian election-interference investigation in good faith, and that the investigation went nowhere because the evidence never appeared — and because most investigations pursue empty leads on a routine basis. It's possible that Strzok is a grandstanding moron with a penchant for grandiosity, particularly when texting his mistress. It's possible that former FBI Director James Comey was radically incompetent at his job.

Which is more likely: that a massive conspiracy took place at the top levels of the FBI and the DOJ to "get Trump" — and that the most damning evidence of Russian collusion, the Trump Tower meeting between Donald Trump Jr. and a Russian government-backed lawyer, didn't emerge until months after the election due to intricate planning? Or that bureaucrats are generally awful at their jobs?

The comfortable thing about conspiracy theories is that they allow us to graft logic onto chaos — they give us a feeling of security. In the words of the Joker in "The Dark Knight," "Nobody panics when things go according to plan, even if the plan is horrifying." But what if there is no plan? What if everybody is just bad at everything? What if the adults who run the most important institutions in the country were the children who picked their noses and put the boogers under the desks in school?

Strzok should have been fired. We should check out all allegations of corruption in government. But our first instinct should usually be to attribute malign acts in government to incompetence rather than malice, because that's usually more accurate.

Do Politics Matter?

August 22, 2018

This week, I bought my wife a present for her birthday: a glass-blowing class. The teacher was, predictably, an eclectically artistic type in Los Angeles, and a down-the-line liberal. As with most conversations these days, the talk turned to President Trump. She quickly let me know her opinion of him (it wasn't high); she then turned to bashing Vice President Mike Pence and Senate Majority Leader Mitch McConnell.

Not once did she raise a policy consideration. Virtually every statement revolved around her personal characterization of political actors — as good people, bad people or indifferent.

I don't think she's out of the mainstream.

There seem to be two main factors in the United States when it comes to voting. Neither has much to do with policy. The first factor is party identification: We tend to vote for the party that shares certain basic policy preferences. The second factor is personal likability of a candidate: We take into account whether we like a candidate or not. Now, these two factors are intertwined: If we like a particular candidate an awful lot, we're likely to identify more with the party of that candidate, and vice versa. This means that a milquetoast candidate's top support number will be the top support number of the party, since the party defines the candidate more than the candidate defines the party (e.g. Mitt Romney). Conversely, a bigger-than-life candidate whose personality seems untethered to the party can lift or drag down the entire party.

That's particularly true with Donald Trump. In today's political environment, your feelings about Trump actually have an impact on how people feel about *you*. Among many conservatives, your support for Trump marks you as a hard-nosed patriot; you're willing to go any distance to defeat the left. If you're among liberals and moderates, your support for Trump marks you as a scurrilous ne'er-do-well who's beneath contempt; you're willing to greenlight any vile behavior so long as you get what you want.

In red or blue districts, this may not matter. But in purple districts, it does. If you have friends on the other side of the aisle, it's uncomfortable to defend Trump's excesses and idiocies. That makes you less likely to openly support Trump, and less likely to support the Republican Party in congressional elections. Presidents who make it difficult to defend them depress turnout in swing districts.

All of which means that if President Trump truly cares about retaining Congress, he has to stop thinking about his base and start thinking about those in the competitive districts. How can he make their lives easier? That's not about policy. At the very least, it's about generating fewer headlines. Trump's base is rock-solid, and it's not going anywhere. But he needs more than his base to win in 2018 and 2020. And barring a personality change, that means minimizing the transaction costs of defending him for those who must show up to the polls.

What Nonreligious People Get Wrong About Religious People

August 29, 2018

With the media furiously obsessed over the supposed imminent end of the Trump presidency (spoiler alert: nope), the new conversation among the elite concerns the supposed evils of Vice President Mike Pence. Pence, our leftist thought leaders proclaim, is perhaps even more frightening than President Trump. Frank Bruni of The New York Times terms Pence a "holy terror waiting in the wings ... a bigot ... a liar ... cruel."

This is nothing new. Conan O'Brien says that "many members of Congress are preparing for a Mike Pence presidency. Yeah, they're preparing by binge-watching 'The Handmaid's Tale.'" Joy Behar called Pence's faith a "mental illness." John Oliver trolled Pence last year by mocking his daughter's children's book about a bunny rabbit — in Oliver's parody book, the bunny rabbit is gay. Because, of course, Pence would *hate* a gay bunny.

Last year, the media went into a tizzy when they learned that Pence refuses to dine alone with women other than his wife (the same media have since been shocked to learn that Harvey Weinstein *loved* dining alone with women other than his wife). This policy made Pence a bigot. But that was just the beginning. Pence, said the media, supported "gay conversion therapy." This, of course, is false as well. But that didn't stop the media from feting gay 2018 Winter Olympian Adam Rippon, who proceeded to trot out that debunked chestnut.

What is so frightening about Pence? His status as a religious Christian. According to many on the left, Pence's religiosity means he's a theocrat. Never mind the fact that Pence is a limited-government conservative who isn't generally interested in imposing policy preferences from above; he believes in The Jesus, and therefore, he must want to install himself at the head of the United Christian States of America.

But that isn't even what bothers those on the left. What bothers many on the left about Pence is the same thing that bothers them about religious Christians in general: They seem convinced that religious Americans are merely bigots hiding behind the Bible. The perspective is well-expressed by Greg Carey, professor of the New Testament at Lancaster Theological Seminary: "People either use religion to justify their bigotry or they refuse to give up their bigotry for the sake of maintaining false religious security." Or let's listen to Bruni again, this time from April 2015: "our debate about religious freedom should include a conversation about freeing religions and religious people from prejudices that they needn't cling to." Or Hillary Clinton in 2016: "deep-seated cultural codes, religious beliefs and structural biases have to be changed."

This view of religious belief is deeply demeaning. The suggestion seems to be that religious texts are utterly malleable, and that human beings twist them to fit their preconceived notions. But the suggestion is alien to most religious people, who believe that their religion dictates and they listen. This perception gap plagues our public discourse and helps explain why the left seems so unperturbed by violating the religious-practice rights of other Americans: They think those Americans are bad human beings using the Bible to shield themselves. Pence is merely the latest example.

The great irony, of course, is that religious people generally wish to be left alone. They're not seeking to impose "The Handmaid's Tale"; such compulsion is endemic to a left that insists we "bake the cake." Such psychological projection damages the public discourse and undermines cultural unity. If the left truly wants a more tolerant America, perhaps it should start by assuming that its opponents in the religious community aren't mere bigots cloaked in the vestments of God — and perhaps it ought to think more deeply about whether the true bigotry lies within itself.

Screaming and Whining Aren't Strategies

September 5, 2018

This week, Democrats pulled out all the stops in their attempts to stop President Trump's pick, Judge Brett Kavanaugh, from gaining a seat on the Supreme Court. Now, Democrats have no power to stop Kavanaugh's ascension; thanks to former Sen. Harry Reid, D-Nev., Democrats invoked the so-called nuclear option in order to reduce the burden for approving judicial nominees down to a simple majority. This has left Democrats and their allies with two options and two options only: screaming and whining.

First, the screaming.

Democratic Sens. Kamala Harris, D-Calif., and Cory Booker, D-N.J., both of whom have already announced they will not support Kavanaugh's nomination, attempted to shut down the Senate Judiciary Committee Kavanaugh hearing. Harris immediately called for an adjournment so that she could supposedly review more of Kavanaugh's documents. Then Booker jumped in. By the end of the first 40 minutes of the hearing, Harris had interrupted eight times; Booker 10 times; Sen. Richard Blumenthal, D-Conn., 13 times; Sen. Mazie Hirono, D-Hawaii, six times; Sen. Amy Klobuchar, D-Minn., three times; Sen. Sheldon Whitehouse, D-R.I., twice; Se. Patrick Leahy, D-Vt. once; and Sen. Chris Coons, D-Del., once. Apparently, all were acting at the behest of Senate Minority Leader Chuck Schumer, D-N.Y., who was attempting to run out the shot clock ... or something.

That was just the beginning. Women's March activist and terrorist sympathizer Linda Sarsour showed up to scream at Republicans; she was arrested. Several more feminist protesters showed up dressed as cast members of "The Handmaid's Tale";

other feminists simply screamed at the top of their lungs during the hearing, forcing their ejection. Planned Parenthood Action tweeted, "This is what the resistance looks like, and we're going to fight like hell to #StopKavanuagh."

The screaming, needless to say, did not work.

And so, the Democrats deployed the next prong of their attack: whining. First, a bevy of leftist commentators on Twitter deployed to inform Americans that Zina Bash, a former Kavanaugh law clerk, was secretly utilizing a white supremacy signal while sitting behind Kavanaugh. Amy Siskind of The Weekly List tweeted, "What fresh hell is this!!!??? Kavanaugh's assistant Zina Bash giving the white power sign right behind him during the hearing? This alone should be disqualify!!!" Eugene Gu, a Twitter celebrity doctor, called the supposed sign a "national outrage and a disgrace to the rule of law." Video of Bash earned millions of views on Twitter within a few hours.

There's only one problem: Bash is half-Mexican and half-Jewish, and her paternal grandparents were Holocaust survivors. Oops.

But more whining was in order. Fred Guttenberg, the father of a Parkland shooting victim, stated that he tried to introduce himself to Kavanaugh but Kavanaugh wouldn't shake his hand. Again, there was only one problem: That never happened. White House deputy press secretary Raj Shah explained: "As Judge Kavanaugh left for his lunch break, an unidentified individual approached him. Before the Judge was able to shake his hand, security had intervened."

Here's the truth: Judicial hearings are largely useless at this point. Thanks to the destruction of Reagan nominee Judge Robert Bork in 1987, judicial nominees know not to answer direct questions about judicial rulings and philosophy, and senators know to only ask questions most likely to land them on television. With that in mind, Senate Majority Leader Mitch McConnell, R-Ky., should simply bring up Kavanaugh for a vote and end this circus.

But he won't. The circus will continue. Our politics will continue to degrade. Anybody who thinks President Trump is the sole performer under the big top should realize that the circus has three rings, and Democrats occupy at least one of them.

When Government Becomes Everything, Everything Becomes Crazy

September 12, 2018

This week, Republican congressional candidate Rudy Peters of California was nearly stabbed by a 35-year-old Castro Valley resident, Farzad Fazeli. According to media reports, Fazeli started shouting about President Trump and then pulled out a switchblade. Thankfully, the switchblade malfunctioned, and Peters was able to fend of Fazeli, who was eventually arrested.

This is far from the only case of political violence we've seen in recent years. The most famous was, of course, the congressional baseball shooting by a crazed Bernie Sanders supporter. House Majority Whip Steve Scalise, R-La., was nearly murdered during the carnage. Now Scalise says: "You've got some people on the left that just want this idea of resist ... you've gotten to where there are death threats and literal attacks on lives ... and frankly, what I want to see is the left stand up against this."

Meanwhile, the right has seen its own violent crazies. Last month, Robert Chain, 68, of California was arrested after allegedly calling The Boston Globe newsroom and threatening to shoot employees. During that call, he called the newspaper the "enemy of the people," echoing the language of President Trump.

So, is the left responsible for Peters? Is President Trump responsible for Chain? Of course not. As always, in a free society, people are responsible for their own actions. Unless a political actor openly calls for violence and that call is heeded, that actor shouldn't be blamed for the violence of acolytes.

With that said, something is deeply wrong.

What's deeply wrong is that we now attribute all failings to the government and all successes to the government. Take, for example, the Washington Post, which suggested in an editorial this week that President Trump is "complicit" about Hurricane Florence because he doesn't support the Post's preferred climate change policy. Now, whatever your feelings about Trump's climate change policy or lack thereof, he's not responsible for a hurricane any more than Barack Obama was responsible for Hurricane Sandy. At best, Trump's policy *may* be contributing to future global warming. But that's not the Post's suggestion. Instead, the Post editors suggest that Trump is himself a King Triton, stirring the seas into hurricane-friendly territory.

By contrast, those on the right suggest that President Trump is solely responsible for our economic boom. They're not wrong to attribute some of the economic growth to consumer confidence and business investment in the wake of Trump's pro-capitalism policies. But Trump isn't any more "in charge" of the economy than Obama was. The economy is far too complex and government is far too complicated for executive tinkering to be attributed to success or blamed for failure.

But we're addicted to our belief in the primal power of our politicians. Once we believe that Trump is either the Great Satan or the Great God, it's no wonder that fringe actors on either side are willing to take extreme measures to harm or "protect" him. The only solution: We must realize that the president is merely a constitutional officer bound by the checks and balances of his role. And we must stop attributing to politics control over our lives that politics does not truly exert.

The Politicization of the Kavanaugh Sexual Abuse Allegations Damages #MeToo

September 19, 2018

This week, Judge Brett Kavanaugh was hit with accusations of sexual abuse from Christine Blasey Ford, a professor at Palo Alto University. According to Ford, some 36 years ago, when Kavanaugh was 17 and she was 15, Kavanaugh took her into a room at a pool party — along with another high school classmate, Mark Judge — and then proceeded to lie on top of her and try to disrobe her, even putting his hand over her mouth to prevent her from screaming.

These are serious allegations. Kavanaugh has denied them completely. He denies he was at such a pool party; he denies he has ever engaged in such behavior. Ford, for her part, only came forward months after sending letters to Sen. Dianne Feinstein, D-Calif., and Rep. Anna Eshoo, D-Calif., and contacting the Washington Post. She originally didn't want to reveal her name or her story. Feinstein didn't ask Kavanaugh about it in writing, or in closed or open hearings; she didn't inform her fellow Democratic senators about the allegations; now she's reportedly attempting to prevent Republican senators from asking questions of Ford.

So, how in the hell is Kavanaugh supposed to defend himself?

This has always been the key question the #MeToo movement has adamantly refused to answer: What should the standard of proof, or even the standard of believability, be? Should the standard be criminal liability? Presumably not, since most accusers are emerging to speak long after alleged incidents. Should the standard be credibility of the individual telling the story combined with supporting details that lend additional credibility? Perhaps, but that apparently isn't enough for some. The standard promoted by many in the #MeToo movement is the far-too-simplistic and outright dangerous "believe all women" standard. By that standard, former President Bill Clinton is a rapist. So are the Duke lacrosse players, the members of a University of Virginia frat house and a foreign exchange Columbia University student — all of whom were exonerated.

Kavanaugh's accuser didn't tell anyone about the incident at the time; she didn't go to the police. Her first retelling of the story came in 2012, three decades after the alleged incident, in a spousal counseling session with a therapist. She told the Washington Post that she doesn't remember key details of the night in question. She doesn't remember the location or how she got there or the date. The notes of her therapist conflict with her statements about the evening.

There are real questions to be asked about her account — and about Feinstein's political maneuvering. But instead, many on the left insist that the "believe all women" standard be applied to accusers against those on the right but that the general credibility standard should be applied to their own favorites. That's nonsensical, and insulting. What's more, it deliberately undermines the bulwark of universal approval with which #MeToo should be met. We should all be able to agree that some standard beyond mere belief is required here — and we should all be willing to hear evidence that implicates our favorite political figures. But if we insist on applying a politically motivated double standard in the name of #MeToo, the support for #MeToo will crumble.

That would be a tragedy, but it would also be a familiar tragedy. All too often, movements that should draw broad public support are undermined by fringe cases used as clubs by members of politically driven groups. We should all agree that any racist police shootings must be stopped — but such agreement falls apart when some insist that questionable shootings be treated as racist shootings. We should all agree that sexual abuse must be stopped — but such agreement disintegrates when some insist that unsubstantiated sexual abuse allegations be treated just like substantiated allegations.

Politics should not be allowed to override basic human decency. Yet again, that's what's happening.

Should You Believe All Accusers?

September 26, 2018

This week, Sen. Ted Cruz, R-Texas, was eating at a restaurant with his wife, Heidi Cruz, when he was suddenly accosted by a group of "anti-racism activists." These activists grilled Sen. Cruz on whether he believed the three-decade-old sexual abuse allegations against Judge Brett Kavanaugh, President Trump's pick to replace former Justice Anthony Kennedy on the Supreme Court. "Do you believe survivors, sir?" one of the protesters asked. The group then began chanting, "We believe survivors!" in increasingly vociferous tones. Eventually, Cruz and his wife were forced to leave the restaurant.

The question was, of course, improperly formed. It assumed facts not in evidence, namely that every allegation against Kavanaugh is true. By labeling all of those making claims "survivors," the protesters simply asserted the conclusion of a case they had yet to make. The question isn't whether one ought to believe "survivors" — of course one should. The question is whether everyone who alleges sexual abuse is, in fact, a survivor of sexual abuse.

And the answer, clearly, is no.

Jackie, a woman who alleged being gang raped at a University of Virginia frat house in the pages of Rolling Stone, leading to a national uproar, was lying. When Emma "Mattress Girl" Sulkowicz was a fourth-year Columbia University student, she alleged that she had been raped by a foreign Columbia student. She was lying. Crystal Mangum alleged that she had been gang raped by members of the Duke lacrosse team. She was lying.

In order for us to determine whom to believe, we must come up with a standard for belief. "Believe all women" just won't cut it, because not all women should be believed. Neither will "innocent until proven guilty," because the court of public opinion isn't a criminal trial. But the answer lies somewhere in between: We should examine the merits of the allegations, the credibility of the accuser, the corroborating evidence. If we fail to do that, we're not actually engaged in fact-finding — we're engaged in confirmation bias.

So, where do we stand with Brett Kavanaugh?

To date, three allegations have been made against Kavanaugh. The first, by a woman named Christine Blasey Ford, seems credible on its face: She says she was at a party with Kavanaugh and his friend, Mark Judge, and that the two of them forced her into a room, where Kavanaugh pressed himself on her, tried to remove her clothes and stifled her screams. But Ford has been less than forthcoming about testifying; has provided no date, time or location of the alleged abuse; and hasn't provided any corroborative evidence. All the witnesses she has cited have denied knowledge of the case.

Then there's Deborah Ramirez, who claims that in college, Kavanaugh thrust his penis in her face at a drunken dormitory party. She told her story to The New Yorker at the behest of Senate Democrats. She freely admitted, as The New Yorker wrote, that "her memories contained gaps because she had been drinking at the time of the alleged incident," and explained that she spent six days "carefully assessing" her memories. No witnesses of the event have come forward. Again, this was at a party.

Finally, there's Julie Swetnick. She came forward via Stormy Daniels' attorney, Michael Avenatti, and claimed that when she and Kavanaugh were in high school, they both went to parties in Maryland during which boys formed "gang rape" lines and spiked the punch with Qualuudes. Swetnick graduated high school three years before Kavanaugh. The story seems incredible on its face.

So, no, it wouldn't be fair to condemn Kavanaugh based on this evidence. Not all accusers are automatically survivors. It's our job to determine whether each individual accusation merits belief. And if the answer is no, that isn't an indicator of sexism. Sometimes it's an indicator than an allegation just doesn't have enough support.

What Do We Have In Common?

October 10, 2018

America stands at a precipice.

It's a moral precipice of our own making: We're not facing any external existential threat, or any serious economic crisis. Nonetheless, we're at each other's throats in a shocking and unique way. At least in the 1960s, serious issues divided us: the national attempt to grapple with legally enshrined racism, the sexual revolution, the Vietnam War. We have no such excuse now. Yet to view the sheer chaos surrounding the confirmation of Justice Brett Kavanaugh is to realize that we may simply have nothing in common anymore, other than our sheer blind luck at having been born into the most prosperous, free, productive country in world history.

But a nation is more than a country. A nation is a people united by history, ideals, culture, institutions. But we've been steadily chipping away at each element of that nationhood.

Our history now divides us. This week, retired astronaut Scott Kelly was forced to apologize on Twitter for the grave sin of quoting Winston Churchill; he tweeted, "I will go and educate myself further on his atrocities, racist views which I do not support." Meanwhile, across America, left-leaning city councils celebrated Indigenous Peoples Day in place of Columbus Day, signaling their belief that Christopher Columbus' discovery of the New World was a tragedy rather than a cause for celebration. We Americans are in the midst of a serious division regarding our own character: Was America and the West founded on fundamentally good and eternal principles, principles we've sometimes failed to live up to, of course, but principles worth fighting for? Or is America and the West the font of evil, the source of suffering, and is all our prosperity merely the fruit of the poisonous tree?

Our ideals divide us, too. On the one hand are "red state" Americans, steeped in traditional Judeo-Christian principles and mores — Americans who believe that our rights are God-given, and that liberty must be balanced by traditional moral virtue. On the other hand are "blue state" Americans, steeped in egalitarian principles and mores — Americans who believe that rights spring from government, and that inequality is a more pressing concern than individual liberty, and that systems of traditional virtue merely mask hierarchical power structures.

Without a shared history or shared ideals, culture and institutions crumble. Our culture has fragmented - can we celebrate July Fourth and stand for the national anthem together, or even watch a football game without arguing about our divisions? Can we attend a movie together without feeling sandbagged by the questions that divide us outside the theater? We certainly no longer attend church or even go bowling together.

And as for institutions, Democrats have now discussed packing the Supreme Court, destroying the Senate and ending the Electoral College thanks to their recent spate of political defeats. All of that follows hard on former President Barack Obama simply arrogating power to himself when he couldn't get Congress to go along with him. Our institutions won't restrain us if we decide to tear ourselves apart.

So, what can hold us together? We can start with gratitude, gratitude for this unique moment in human history, for our unique country, for our unique ideals, for our unique institutions. If we're ungrateful, spite will win the day. And that means that we could be setting the charges for a spectacular implosion.

Democrats Know They Can Always Count on the Media

October 17, 2018

This week, Sen. Elizabeth Warren, D-Mass., in preparation for a 2020 presidential run, decided to fight back against President Trump's brutal nickname for her: Pocahontas. Trump, you'll recall, labeled her Pocahontas because for years, she has claimed Native American ancestry. Not only that, she claimed repeatedly that her mother's Native American ancestry drove her parents to elope after her father's family refused to welcome her mother with open arms thanks to their bigotry. As it turns out, Warren could never provide any evidence of Native American ancestry — even though she spent years labeling herself Native American while at the University of Pennsylvania Law School as well as Harvard Law School.

On Monday, Warren decided she'd had enough. She released a video of her family members discussing her claims of Native American background. "Native communities have faced discrimination, neglect and violence for generations," Warren intoned. "And Trump can say whatever he wants about me, but mocking Native Americans or any group in order to try to get at me? That's not what America stands for."

She accompanied that video with her supposed proof of Native American background: an analysis by professor Carlos Bustamante of Stanford University in which he explains that it is *possible* that Warren had a Native American ancestor anywhere from six to 10 generations ago. That would have made her anywhere from 1/64 to 1/1,024 Native American. The study was based not on Native American DNA but on Mexican, Peruvian and Colombian DNA.

In fact, not even Cherokees were happy with Warren. In a stunning rebuke, the Cherokee Nation released a statement saying, "Senator Warren is undermining tribal interests with her continued claims of tribal heritage," and that Warren's DNA test "makes a mockery out of DNA tests and its legitimate uses while also dishonoring legitimate tribal governments and their citizens, whose ancestors are well documented and whose heritage is proven."

All of this should have been foreseeable by anyone with half a brain. Falsely claiming you are Native American for years is bad enough. But releasing a study demonstrating that you are 99.9 percent white — and then claiming that such a study justifies your false claims? What made Warren, an intelligent human being, think such a thing?

Only one simple fact: Warren knows, as everyone in politics knows, that the media will cover for nearly any instance of leftist political manipulation. They'll cover for Warren fibbing about her ancestry. They'll cover for Texas Senate candidate Beto O'Rourke driving drunk, plowing into a truck and then attempting to flee the scene of the crime. They'll cover for Arizona Senate candidate Rep. Kyrsten Sinema saying that she didn't care if Americans joined the Taliban (CNN's headline: "Kyrsten Sinema's Anti-War Activist Past Under Scrutiny as She Runs for Senate"). Democrats have the enviable advantage of being able to trot out nearly any story and be given credibility by most of the mainstream media.

Non-Democrats, however, see this game. And every time the media simply parrot Democratic talking points on issues like Warren's ancestry, they undercut their credibility. Large media institutions have done more than anyone, including President Trump, to destroy their reputations with the American people. Their pathetic behavior over the past few weeks, in the approach to the 2018 elections, shows that they're doubling down on stupid.

How Democrats Learned to Stop Worrying and Love Federalism

October 24, 2018

In today's polarized political environment, I'm often asked how I think America can come back together. My answer is pretty simple: we learn to leave each other alone. I didn't like President Obama much; folks on the left don't like President Trump. I wanted President Obama and Democrats interfering as little as possible in my life; Democrats presumably feel the same about President Trump and the Republicans. So, here's a solution: the founders' solution. It's called checks and balances, federalism and localism.

For too long, the Democratic Party has operated under a certain assumption: The tides of history are in its favor. Aggregation of power to the federal government, usurpation of power by the judiciary, centralization of power in the executive branch — all of that would redound to their political benefit. And for decades, they were largely correct: Not only did the federal government continue to grow but federal policymaking also shifted consistently leftward, with brief points of stagnation during eras of Republican rule.

But President Trump's ascension to power has shocked the Democrats awake. Suddenly, some Democrats have realized that they are not fated to rule forever — and that powers handed to the federal government by Democrats can be turned against Democrats, too.

This shock has resulted in two Democratic responses. The first: a determination to change the system of government itself to forestall any future Republican victory. Thus, we've heard calls to abolish the Electoral College (not happening), to pack the Supreme Court (not happening), to apportion the Senate based on population (not happening). The second response, however, is more tenable and far more appealing across the political aisle: a restoration of the founding promise to devolve authority to local authorities.

This week, Hillary Clinton hit upon this unique strategy — a strategy some centuries old but fought tooth and nail by the left — seemingly by accident. She tweeted, "A reality of a Supreme Court with a right-wing majority is that the states are a new important front in protecting civil rights — especially the rights of the most vulnerable among us."

The states aren't that new. They've been around for a couple of centuries, and they've always been designed to protect the interests of local populations. Sometimes those interests have been brutal and terrible — see, for example, slavery and Jim Crow — but sometimes those interests have been positive and welcome. In designing a system determined to please the greatest number of human beings, localism is usually, but not invariably, the solution. As James Madison wrote in Federalist No. 39, our government is "neither wholly national nor wholly federal." There's a reason for that.

It's good to see members of the left finally discovering some founding philosophy. But there is one problem with the left's view of federalism and devolution of power: That view seems temporary. The minute Democrats seize power once more, the glories of federalism will surely recede into the background in favor of the club of federal power. That's just one more reason that Democrats shouldn't be handed that power anytime soon.

When We Broaden the Definition of Incitement, Freedom Suffers

October 31, 2018

Over the past week, we've heard the media pitching one particular narrative nonstop: the story that President Donald Trump's rhetoric has resulted in increased violence. We heard it in the aftermath of a spate of attempted bombing attacks against Democratic targets by a Floridian nut job, and we heard it in the aftermath of a shooting attack on a Pittsburgh synagogue by an outspokenly anti-Trump white supremacist.

Is there truth to the charge?

To determine whether there is, we've first got to consider the question more broadly: When is speech related to violence?

It's obvious that speech is often related to action. We change how we think and see the world based on what other people say to us. We change our opinions. Our emotions can be soothed or our anger provoked. The entire purpose of political speech is to motivate people to believe and act in certain ways. It would be foolish and shortsighted to suggest, then, that over-the-top rhetoric and violent metaphor have *no* impact on the public discourse.

But we cannot equate all speech with incitement, obviously. To do so would be to destroy the entire rationale for free speech. If we can attribute the violence of a few to the speech of public figures, the only available solution would be to curtail speech. And we cannot base our standard for protected speech on those with eggshell skulls. If the craziest and most easily provoked among us become the standard, then free speech dies.

Thus, our legal system generally relies on a "reasonable person" standard when determining whether speech incites action. Courts of appeal have held that threats and incitement generally require that "a reasonable person would foresee that the statement would be interpreted by those to whom the maker communicates the statement as a serious expression of an intention to inflict bodily injury."

By this standard, none of President Trump's statements has come close to inciting either attempted bombings or shootings. The media's suggestions otherwise seem to equate speech with violence, making an argument for moral culpability that cannot be sustained.

But that doesn't mean that misuse of non-inciting free speech isn't damaging. It most certainly is. Rhetoric that equates political opposition with murderers, traitors or enemies of the people tears away at the social fabric, the base-line trust we have for one another. If our opponents are motivated by evil intent, then why bother conversing with them? If they're deplorables on the one hand and globalists who intend to destroy the country on the other, how are we supposed to come together in civil ways?

The answer is that we won't. And every violent act merely tears us apart further as we seek to cast blame on those we think either inspired or supported the violent act. Lone evil actors can kill and maim. Only we, as a country, can tear ourselves apart. And as we blame one another for the actions of non-reasonable actors, we're doing just that.

The Myth of Obama, the Myth of Trump and the Reality of Elections

November 7, 2018

In the aftermath of this week's midterm elections, in which Democrats gained 34 House seats and lost an additional three Senate seats, an odd emotional disconnect took place. Democrats, who had just won control of the House, seemed disappointed in their victory; they had expected a sweeping tsunami to carry them from Arizona across Texas and through Florida. They seemed borderline despondent that their extraordinarily dislike for President Trump hadn't translated into historic gains. Meanwhile, Republicans, who had just surrendered the speakership to Nancy Pelosi, were somewhat giddy; they immediately paid homage to President Trump for his stunning work in preventing Democrats from marking up big wins in Florida and Ohio.

All of this seems somewhat misguided.

The disparate reactions of the two political parties are predicated on a foundational myth about modern American politics: the myth of Barack Obama. According to the Obama Myth, once upon a time, America was divided between red and blue on the basis of right-left politics. Then, along came President Obama, who won two sweeping electoral victories, forging a coalition of intersectional identity groups in emergent demographic groups and utterly reshaping the electoral map in a permanent way.

For Democrats, the Obama Myth leads them to see President Trump's 2016 as an electoral aberration — a momentary spasm of the American public, soon to be corrected. Any indicator that 2016 was more of a trend than an outlier cuts against the Obama Myth.

For Republicans, the Obama Myth leads them to believe in the Trump Myth. The Trump Myth suggests that once upon a time, there was a land dominated by an intersectional coalition set to rule in perpetuity. Then along came Donald Trump, who broke apart the blue wall and set in its place a new movement, populist and deep. This myth portrays President Trump as an electoral magician, a man defying gravity and leading Republicans into uncharted new lands of victory. Its adherents become willing to attribute every victory to Trump and every loss to lack of Trump — a theory Trump actively promotes by slamming Republican politicians who fail to embrace him sufficiently.

But here's the thing: The Obama Myth is a myth, and so is the Trump Myth. The reality is that the electoral aberration was not Trump but Obama. Trump isn't a magician; he's a regression to the electoral mean. Here are the percentages of the vote won by Republican presidential candidates in 2000, 2004, and 2016 in Ohio: 50.0, 50.8, 51.3. Here are those numbers for Florida: 48.9, 52.1, 48.6. For Wisconsin: 47.6, 49.3, 47.2. For Pennsylvania: 46.4, 48.5, 48.2. For Michigan: 46.1, 47.8, 47.3.

Trump didn't significantly overperform in any of these states. He did what Republicans, absent Obama, did in 2004 and 2000.

What, then, was 2016? 2016 was an odd combination of a regression to the Republican mean and Hillary Clinton's incredible incompetence, as well as low Democratic turnout thanks to their belief that she would surely win. That's why we shouldn't be surprised by last night's results. Republicans performed as they've always performed outside of Obama. Democrats performed as they've always performed outside Obama.

So, what lesson should Republicans learn? That political gravity applies to President Trump — and that they've got to reach out to the suburban voters they lost in the midterms. What lesson should Democrats learn? The Republican Party remains competitive in swing states, and running to the hard progressive left while shouting about Trump won't cut it.

Will either party learn those lessons? Probably not. So buckle up. It's going to be a wild two years.

Nationalism and Patriotism Don't Have to Be Opposites

November 14, 2018

On Sunday, French President Emmanuel Macron spoke at a ceremony marking the 100th anniversary of the end of World War I. There, he took the opportunity to slam President Trump's "America First" nationalism. "Patriotism," Macron said, "is the exact opposite of nationalism: Nationalism is a betrayal of patriotism. By putting our interests first, with no regard for others, we erase the very thing that a nation holds dearest, and the thing that keeps it alive: its moral values."

This statement has a sort of European charm. It's also false. And dangerous.

Nationalism, when opposed to patriotism, can indeed be terrible. It can suggest that the interests of one nation override the interests of every other nation, that imperialism and colonialism are worth pursuing out of love of blood and soil. But when combined with patriotism, nationalism can also be a bulwark against tyranny. Nationalism can stand up to international communism. Nationalism can refuse to bow before the dictates of multiculturalism, which suggest that all cultures and practices are of equal value.

Patriotism is a philosophy of national values: It is a statement that your nation has values that are eternal, true and noble. American patriotism prizes God-given individual rights protected by limited government. Were America to lose God-given individual rights protected by limited government, it would no longer be America. But patriotism doesn't mean that it is the job of America to spread our values everywhere else to the detriment of our own national strength. Our patriotism encompasses American nationalism: We believe that America must come first so that America can be strong enough to promote her values where appropriate.

It is simply a fact that human beings resonate to nationalism. The question is whether that nationalism can be grafted to a worthwhile philosophy. The German troops of World War I marched into battle out of national pride; so, too, did the American doughboys. Americans have fought and died for their flag and their families; so have soldiers of other nations. But America is great because that flag stands for certain values, and American families are built on those values.

The opposite of nationalism, then, isn't patriotism. It's internationalism, or the idea that all human beings share similar values, and that, therefore, borders and national interests are irrelevant. That philosophy is utterly foolish and dangerous. Simply view tape of thousands of radical Muslims marching in Pakistan to protest the acquittal of a Christian woman from charges of blasphemy and realize that not all people believe the same things.

But that multicultural philosophy has led Europe to open her borders to waves of migrants who may not share European values, and who have led to cultural polarization and, indeed, the rise of right-wing nationalist movements. It's that philosophy that has led Europe to leave behind her uniquely Western heritage in favor of a broader outlook that has undermined her cultural solidarity.

Nationalism, then, isn't the problem. Lack of values is. And mistaking anti-nationalism for a value system in and of itself endangers free citizens who hold worthwhile national values dear.

The Ungrateful Nation

November 21, 2018

Here are a few facts about America.

The unemployment rate among those with a high school education is 3.9 percent. The poorest quintile of Americans have seen their post-tax incomes increase 80 percent since 1979, according to Congressional Budget Office data, and post-tax and transfer income for that quintile has skyrocketed 32 percent since 2000. The upper-middle class in America constituted 13 percent of the population in 1979; as of 2014, it constituted 30 percent. According to Pew Research from 2015, when it comes to standard of living, "The U.S. stands head and shoulders above the rest of the world. More than half (56 percent) of Americans were high income by the global standard ... and 2 percent were poor."

Fantastic products are cheaper than ever. Human Progress investigated the amount of time Americans must spend to earn enough money to buy key products and found that since 1979, the amount of time spent to earn a refrigerator had dropped 52 percent, 95 percent for microwaves, 65 percent for gas ranges and 61 percent for dishwashers. Between the mid-1960s and 2007, Americans were able to work less and leisure more: They worked nearly eight hours fewer per week, according to The Heritage Foundation. The wage gap is almost entirely a myth: Women who work the same jobs as men for the same number of hours, and have the same work history and same education as men make the same as men. The chief obstacles to income mobility in the United States are related to personal decision-making, not racial discrimination: As the Brookings Institution points out, of the people who finish high school, get a full-time job and wait until age 21 to get married and have children, nearly 75 percent join the middle class, and just 2 percent remain in poverty.

What of freedom? In America, people of all religions practice freely, so long as the government isn't attempting to cram social justice down on them. People are free to speak, so long as government actors aren't utilizing the heckler's veto. We are free to use the press, free to associate and free to protest.

All of this is the result of the greatest governmental philosophy ever committed to paper: God-given individual rights protected by limited government. We haven't always lived up to that philosophy — in some areas, we've progressed mightily, and in others, we've regressed. But the overall success of the United States should be ringing proof that at the very least, we should be grateful and proud to live here.

Yet as of July 2018, fewer than half of Americans surveyed by Gallup said they are extremely proud to be American. Just 32 percent of Democrats, down from 56 percent in 2013, said they are extremely proud to be American; only 42 percent of independents said are were extremely proud to be American. That's ridiculous. Regardless of political affiliation, we should be proud to live in a society founded on eternal truths, in which we have the ability to thrive based on our own choices.

In 1789, as America struggled to find her footing after a revolution against the most powerful military and economic engine in the world, then-President George Washington issued a proclamation. He thanked God for "his kind care and protection of the People of this Country," for "the great degree of tranquility, union, and plenty, which we have since enjoyed — for the peaceable and rational manner, in which we have been enabled to establish constitutions of government for our safety and happiness."

If Washington could urge gratefulness in 1789, we'd be fools not to do so now, when our lives are so much better in every material way. This Thanksgiving, let's remember what we have — and let's remember the eternal ideas that provide the groundwork for our prosperity.

'Medicare-for-All' Is No Health Care Cure-All

November 28, 2018

This week, congresswoman-elect Alexandria Ocasio-Cortez, D-N.Y., tweeted out a letter from Spectrum Health to one Hedda Elizabeth Martin. The letter described the clinic's rejection of a heart transplant for Martin based on lack of a "more secure financial plan for immunosuppressive medication coverage." The clinic added, "The Committee is recommending a fundraising effort of $10,000." Ocasio-Cortez tweeted, "Insurance groups are recommending GoFundMe as official policy — where customers can die if they can't raise the goal in time — but sure, single payer healthcare is unreasonable."

First off, Ocasio-Cortez is simply incorrect. The letter itself isn't directly from the insurance company but from the clinic. It declined to perform the heart surgery because the patient didn't have the ability to pay for the medications necessary to prevent organ rejection by the immune system. Furthermore, deductibles on insurance that would cover such drugs under Obamacare would certainly surpass the $10,000 requested by the clinic.

Most of all, though, Martin's health care was provided, in this case, by Medicare Part B. She herself explained via a since-deleted post on Facebook: "with my 20 percent copay for pharmaceuticals under Part B ... it will cost me about $700 a month for my part B copay for anti-rejection drugs. Once I reach my $4500 annual my cost is $0. So they want me to show I can cover my $4500 deductible by saving $10,000 ... which I will do."

So, would "Medicare-for-all" — Ocasio-Cortez's preferred solution — actually take care of the problem? Or would it exacerbate it, given that nationalized health care creates *more* rationing, not less? There's a reason nationalized health care systems like Sweden's and Britain's have necessitated increased private spending *outside* of the rationed systems. As Scott Atlas of the Hoover Institution points out: "Sweden has increased its spending on private care for the elderly by 50 percent in the past decade, abolished its government's monopoly over pharmacies, and made other reforms. Last year alone, the British government spent more than $1 billion on care from private and other non-NHS providers."

And the entire global medical industry benefits from America's private health care spending, which drives the creation of new drugs. So what happens when America no longer covers the cost for such pharmaceuticals? Our Food and Drug Administration may be slow, but it's a lot faster than its European equivalents, which is why the vast majority of new cancer drugs are developed and made available faster in the United States.

In the end, Martin did go to GoFundMe to raise $20,000, not the requisite $10,000. In less than two days, she raised nearly $30,000 from over 400 people. GoFundMe may not be scalable for everyone — but neither is "Medicare-for-all," which is why California scrapped the proposed state version for fear of doubling the budget. Better access to high-quality health care can only be made a reality by an increase in supply, not demand; through innovation, not regulation; through incentivization, not cramdowns. And that means that all of the fulminating over "Medicare-for-all" misses the point and often hangs those most in need out to dry.

Policies Have Consequences

December 5, 2018

This week, France set itself on fire; the stock market tumbled; and news broke that low-wage employment tumbled in the city of Seattle. What do these three headlines have in common? That policies aren't wish lists — they have real-world consequences.

Begin in France, where the so-called "yellow vests" — a group of anti-tax protesters dressed in safety vests — tore up Paris. Rioters defaced the Arc de Triomphe, burned cars and attacked police with stones. They were protesting the exorbitant fuel taxes pursued by French President Emmanuel Macron, taxes designed to curb climate change. The fuel tax rates in France are already estimated to be a whopping 64 percent on unleaded fuel and 59 percent on diesel fuel. The riots resulted in the French government backing down, with French Prime Minister Edouard Philippe announcing, "No tax is worth putting in danger the unity of the nation." By polling data, more than 70 percent of French voters support the yellow vests, and Macron's approval rating has dropped to an anemic 23 percent.

Move to the United States, where the stock market continued to experience outsized volatility this week — volatility increased by the hot-and-cold pronouncements of President Trump on trade. On Monday, thanks in part to optimistic pronouncements on the postponement of a trade war with China, the Dow Jones Industrial Average rose more than 250 points. On Tuesday, President Trump tweeted that he favors protectionism, dubbing himself "a Tariff Man," and the stock market promptly plummeted more than 600 points. It turns out that talking up the economic benefits of domestic taxation of consumers doesn't do much for consumer confidence or investor optimism.

Now take a look at Seattle, where a new analysis from economists at the University of Washington shows that the city's forced $15 minimum wage had resulted in serious consequences for low-wage workers. The study found that the costs to low-wage workers outpaced benefits "by a ratio of three to one," according to the Washington Post, amounting to an average of $125 per month lost to the average low-wage worker.

But no matter: So long as there are politicians, there will be policies that achieve the opposite of their intended consequences. Politicians, after all, don't have to show results. All they have to demonstrate is a willingness to "help." Thus, the G-20 last year announced that carbon taxes would offer "significant opportunities for modernizing our economies" — workers be damned. President Trump has declared that tariffs are an economic winner, despite reams of evidence to the contrary. And Rep.-elect Alexandria Ocasio-Cortez proclaims that we mustn't "whine about minimum wage" — if we don't implement a minimum wage, we will only be paying "human labor less than they require to live."

Policies have real-world consequences, regardless of how much we wish they don't. It's failure to cope with that basic fact that leads to so much of the finger-pointing we see in politics, with each side accusing the other of bad intention — as though pointing out a policy's failure is equivalent to rooting for failure. It isn't. But rooting for reality is a far more sustainable economic strategy than fighting against it.

The 'International Community'
Isn't a Community

December 12, 2018

Very often these days, we hear about the wonderful richness of the international community. Americans are chastised for failing to go along with the international community on climate change; failing to follow the consensus of the international community on health care; failing to mirror the priorities of the international community in foreign policy.

But here's the reality: There is no international community. There is merely a group of states motivated by self-interest. Sometimes those self-interests overlap. Other times they don't. But let's not pretend that the international community somehow maintains a sort of collective moral standing merely by dint of numbers. In fact, precisely the opposite is often true.

Take, for example, the United Nations' recent decision not to condemn the Palestinian terrorist group Hamas. This week, the U.N. General Assembly voted on a resolution condemning the group for "repeatedly firing rockets into Israel and for inciting violence, thereby putting civilians at risk," as well as for using assets to construct "tunnels to infiltrate Israel and equipment to launch rockets into civilian areas." The U.N., which requires a two-thirds vote to pass a General Assembly resolution, voted down the resolution — 87 nations in favor, 58 against, 32 abstaining. All in all, that means that more nations voted against ratifying the resolution — 90 — than in favor of it.

Up to this point, the U.N. has never passed a single resolution against Hamas.

Just days later, Palestinian terrorists opened fire on a group of people waiting for a bus near Ofra, a settlement in Judea and Samaria. The drive-by shooting wounded seven people, including a pregnant woman and her unborn child, as well as her husband. Both the woman and the baby are now in critical condition; it will be a miracle if both survive. According to The Times of Israel, Hamas immediately praised the attack, deeming it "heroic" and an "affirmation of our people's choice and legitimacy in resisting the Zionist occupation and its settlers."

Hamas isn't hiding the ball. It is evil. It celebrates evil. It pays terrorists to commit acts of evil. But the international community isn't hiding the ball either when its members refuse to condemn terrorism as terrorism when it is directed against disfavored members of the international community.

Take, by contrast, the international community's reaction to a terrorist attack directed against an Iranian military parade in late September. The U.N. Security Council forcibly condemned the attack, calling it a "heinous and cowardly terrorist attack" and pledging its support to "hold perpetrators, organizers, financiers and sponsors of these reprehensible acts of terrorism accountable and bring them to justice."

What's the difference? Only the perpetrators and the targets. The international community is a joke. Perhaps the United States ought to change its climate change or health care or gun policies. But those arguments should never be made on the basis of the international standard of morality — a standard that doesn't exist, has never existed and ought not be the subject of pretending by Western nations that ought to know better.

The Left's War on Parenting

December 19, 2018

Last month, the New York State Education Department made a crucial decision: Commissioner MaryEllen Elia handed authority to local school boards to veto the right for private schools to operate. Those school boards must now determine whether private schools provide an education "substantially equivalent to that received in district public schools." According to Jewish educators Elya Brudny and Yisroel Reisman, "The state government now requires private schools to offer a specific set of classes more comprehensive than what students in public schools must learn." This isn't a problem for Jewish schools alone — Catholic schools in New York have bucked the legislation, with James Cultrara, executive secretary of the New York Council of Catholic School Superintendents, explaining, "We simply cannot accept a competing school having authority over whether our schools can operate."

Now there's a case to be made that the state has an interest in children learning basic secular studies, and to that end, Cultrara has called for an objective standard for evaluating whether or not schools are properly educating their students. That case is far stronger in a welfare state, in which insufficient education often ends with the public bearing the brunt of such failures.

But there's also a case to be made that parents are the best sources for judging which educational standards their children should obtain — and that attempting to force-feed education to unwilling students and parents at threat of legal peril is a massive imposition on freedom. It's also unlikely that a broadly applied standard of education will succeed in raising standards across the board. The public school system hasn't been able to achieve that even absent religious conflicts.

More fascinating than this debate, however, is the generalized attitude toward parenting expressed by the social left. If you choose to send your child to a non-approved yeshiva, you must be policed and your child threatened with truancy. If, however, you are a parent who decides to expose your 11-year-old son to risk of sexual perversion, then you're open-minded and noble.

What else are we to take from the story of Desmond Napoles? Napoles is an 11-year-old boy who dresses in drag for national press, and who was squired — presumably by his parents — to a gay bar in Brooklyn, New York, called 3 Dollar Bill, where grown men proceeded to hand dollar bills to him. As writer Matt Walsh has pointed out, were Desmond a girl being paraded by her parents before the leering stares of grown men, child protective services would be called. But since Desmond is a celebrity who has been exploited by his parents, this is all worth celebrating.

Which is, perhaps, one of the reasons so many religious parents don't want the state of New York determining what they should and should not be allowed to teach their children. Religious parents may look at the world created by the social left and say that they want to inculcate in their children an alternative set of values. There may be costs to that. Perhaps there are ways to mitigate those costs. But overall, only one set of parents is being punished for making "educational" decisions by the state of New York — and it's not the set of parents cross-dressing their pre-pubescent children for fun and cash.

About the Author

Ben Shapiro was born in 1984. He entered the University of California Los Angeles at the age of 16 and graduated summa cum laude and Phi Beta Kappa in June 2004 with a Bachelor of Arts degree in Political Science. He graduated Harvard Law School cum laude in June 2007.

Shapiro was hired by Creators Syndicate at age 17 to become the youngest nationally syndicated columnist in the United States. His columns are printed in major newspapers and websites including *The Riverside Press-Enterprise* and the *Conservative Chronicle*, Townhall.com, ABCNews.com, WorldNetDaily.com, Human Events, FrontPageMag.com, and FamilySecurityMatters.com. His columns have appeared in *The Christian Science Monitor, Chicago Sun-Times, Orlando Sentinel, The Honolulu Advertiser, The Arizona Republic, Claremont Review of Books,* and RealClearPolitics.com. He has been the subject of articles by *The Wall Street Journal, The New York Times*, The Associated Press, and *The Christian Science Monitor*. He has been quoted on "The Rush Limbaugh Show" and "The Dr. Laura Show," at CBSNews.com, and in the *New York Press, The Washington Times*, and *The American Conservative*.

Shapiro is the author of best-sellers *Brainwashed: How Universities Indoctrinate America's Youth, Porn Generation: How Social Liberalism Is Corrupting Our Future*, and *Project President: Bad Hair and Botox on the Road to the White House*. He has appeared on hundreds of television and radio shows around the nation, including *The O'Reilly Factor, Fox and Friends, In the Money, DaySide with Linda Vester, Scarborough Country, The Dennis Miller Show, Fox News Live, Glenn Beck Show, Your World with Neil Cavuto, 700 Club, The Laura Ingraham Show, The Michael Medved Show, The G. Gordon Liddy Show, The Rusty Humphries Show, "The Lars Larson Show, The Larry Elder Show, The Hugh Hewitt Show*, and *The Dennis Prager Show*.

Shapiro is married and runs Benjamin Shapiro Legal Consulting in Los Angeles.

Whining Doesn't Win
is also available as an e-book
for Kindle, Amazon Fire, iPad, Nook and
Android e-readers. Visit
creatorspublishing.com to learn more.

o o o

CREATORS PUBLISHING

We publish books.
We find compelling storytellers and
help them craft their narrative,
distributing their novels and collections
worldwide.

o o o

Made in the USA
Monee, IL
03 February 2021